Influences on RABINDRANATH TAGORE

Sanjeev Sharma

RAJAT PUBLICATIONS
New Delhi

Influences on Rabindranath Tagore
by *Sanjeev Sharma*

This edition is published by Rajat Publications
4740/23, Ansari Road Daryaganj,
New Delhi - 110002

ISBN: 978-81-7880-503-0

Edition 2025

Printed and bound in India

RAJAT
PUBLICATIONS

4740/23, Ansari Road, Daryaganj,
New Delhi- 110002 (India)
Mob:- +91-9811484973, +91-9811105389
E-mail: rajat_publication@yahoo.com

Preface

The present study is an attempt to scrutinise closely the creative and expository writings of Tagore and also the various studies made on him with a view to establishing the major influences which shaped the mind and art of this most celebrated Indian creative artist of the modern age. A great genius like that of his is essentially and fundamentally original and his writings are primarily founded on his initiative understanding and experiences of life and art; but it does not imply that he did not learn anything from his illustrious predecessors and contemporaries. The truth is that numerous Indian and foreign influences worked in his actively, and prominently contributed to the making of his art and ideas. He was fully conversant with, and equally at home among, the thinkers and writers of the East and the West. In fact, he belonged both to the East and the West, and he proclaimed it by remarking that his name 'Rabi', which meant the sun, fully explained it, because like the sun he rose in the East but travelled and belonged to the West as much.

Thus, it should not look absurd and amazing if scholars draw parallels between his masterpieces and those of the great artists of the world of all categories, such as the composers of the *vedic* literature, Kalidas, Vaishnava poets, Kabir, Hafiz, the great Greeks, Sappho, Shakespeare, Milton, Wordsworth, Byron, Shelley, Keats, Tennyson, Browning, Rossetti, Francis Thompson, Heine, Tolstoy, Dostoevsky, Walt Whitman, Kipling, W.B. Yeats, Ezra Pund, T.S. Elito and many others. But the truth is that he is not like this author or that, but is Rabindranath Tagore, who is strikingly unique and original in his own way in that in him all the best streams of thoughts merge into one losing their independent entities completely and are given a new colouring by his extraordinary innate genius.

– Author

Contents

1

Early Influences: The Bengal of Rabindranath Tagore's Times and His Family Background

The life, literature and culture of the Bengal of Rabindranath Tagore's times greatly shaped his creative mind and art. The *Mahabharata* refers to the ancient Dravidian tribes that inhabited Bengal, and makes a mention of five brothers—Ang, Bang, Kaling, Pundra and Sushama—belonging to these tribes which were fairly civilized and had a definite culture of their own. With the passage of time, some tribes from Tibet and China migrated to Bengal and settled down there in the pre-Christian and pre-Aryan era. Though Kautilya's *Arthashastra,* believed to have been written in the fourth century B.C., speaks high of the silk and other fine articles manufactured by the ancient Bengali people, yet Bengal is not proud of having any literary work in any of the non-Aryan languages. The Aryan language had its earliest impact on Bengal between 1500 to 500 B.C., and with this a new civilization came into being in Bengal. But it was during the Gupta period of Indian history that Bengal underwent a great change, both linguistically and culturally. By the seventh century Sanskrit and Prakrit swayed Bengal, and the modern Bengal can be said to be the product of the impact of the Aryan language and culture.

However, by the eleventh century Bengal had developed its own distinct culture and language. Thus as early as around 1159 Sarvanand, a Bengali Pandit, brought out an annotation of *Amar Kosh,* which is attached significance in that the non-Sanskrit words used in it give us an idea of the old Bengali language. Of the ancient Bengali literature, Charyapad, a collection of Bengali songs of the saints of Sahajiya Panth between the twelfth and the fourteenth century, is very significant in asmuch as it surely influenced the people of Bengal of later centuries and must have moulded the cultural and literary facets of Rabindranath's personality. But more than this ancient collection of songs, the writings and poems of *'Prakrit Pengal'* and Jayadeva's *Gitgovinda* contributed to the growth of Bengali literature and language. Many of the lyrics of Tagore obviously evince the tradition of the love poetry launched by Jayadeva in his very popular masterpiece, which is usually believed to have been originally composed in ancient Bengali towards the and of the twelfth country. Two more works of old Bengali—*Dakarnay* abounding in the suggestions of Charvaka philosophy, and the poetical compositions of Khana related to Agriculture—deserve our attention, for they, it is commonly believed by the scholars of Bengali literature, exerted influence on the writers of modern Bengali literature, and naturally Tagore must not have escaped this influence.

Hinduism and Buddhism have been the two quite prominent influences on the life and literature of Bengal. Buddhism dominated Bengal only for a short period, and therefore many works of Buddhism were converted into Hindu religious books, and Lord Buddha was presented as Lord Shiva in them. The distinguished early Bengali poets with whom Tagore was fully familiar, directly or indirectly, were Ramai Pandit, the writer of *Shunya Purana,* Mayur Bhatt, Durlabh Malik and others. Thus Tagore imbibed the essence of Buddhism—compassion and love—and Hinduism—the *Shaiv, Shakti* and *Vaishnava* traditions—and gave full expression to it in his writings.

Another conspicuous influence on modern Bengali poets, including Rabindranath Tagore, has been that of Chandidas and Vidyapati The former is regarded as the first major Bengali poet. Known as 'mad Chandi' because of his love for Rani, a washerwoman, this priest of a temple wrote songs to celebrate his love for his beloved, though the basic theme of his poetry is obviously the love of Lord Krishna and Radha. As popular in Bengal as Surdas in Hindi region, his poetry is first rate and is comparable with the best in any language. Vidyapati, who belonged to Mithila, has always been very popular in Bengal. Rabindranath Tagore's poetry reverberates with the echoes of the best of Vidyapati.

Bengali poetry is essentially religious, often drawing themes and ideas from the *Puranas*, the *Ramayana*, the *Mahabharata*, the *Upanishads*, etc., and Rabindranath Togore's writings are not an exception to it. Born in 1346, Krativas was the first to write *Saptkand Ramayana* in Bengali poetry on the request of the king of Gaur. The first *Mahabharata* in Bengali was written by Sanjay, contemporary of Krativas. Some later Bengali versions of the *Mahabharata* came out from the pens of authors like Nasarat Khan, Parameshwar and Kasiram Das. Undoubtedly, these two great epics of India have exerted tremendous impact on the cultural life of Bengal and on the writings of Rabindranath Tagore.

Rabindranath Tagore was much benefitted by some of the celebrated Bengali poets of the nineteenth century. Innovator of a new form of poetry called *Panchali*, Daharathi Rai occupies a unique place among these poets. But the credit of delinking poetry from religion goes to Nidhi Babu, whose actual name was Ramanidhi Gupta. However, Michael Madhusudan Dutt, acknowledged as the Valmiki of Bengal, was the greatest Bengali poet of this period. A highly learned man, well-versed in European languages and literatures, he became a Christian on account of his love for a Christian lady. He gave a new turn and dimension to Bengali poetry by bringing it very close to Western literature. His *magnum opus, Meghanadvadh,* is a previous possession of Bengali poetry. But it was Viharilal Chakravarty, a lesser genius, whom Rabindranath Tagore proclaimed as his literary master, whose poetry is simple and refreshingly inspiring and hence possesses a great appeal for the masses. His best–known books are *Sardamangal, Bandhu Viyog, Sangeet-Satak* and *Prem Pravahani.* Tagore's immediate predecessors were Surendranath Majumdar, Devendranath Sen and Akshaya Kumar Barhal. The first of these was mostly engaged in rendering poems of other languages into Bengali, and composed only a little good original poetry.

But more formidable than all this was the influence of Maharshi Devendranath, Dwijendranath and Jyotirindranath on Rabindranath. All the three – the father and the elder brothers – were creative artists with outstanding literary sensibilities. They would discuss literary and other matters for hours together and young Rabindranath would listen to them attentively. This small literary circle was often attended by some other literary luminaries of that time, such as Akshay Chandra Chaudhury and Viharilal. While Jyoti always inspired him to go to, and participate, in the musical parties and literary discussions, Akshay Chandra, who was saturated with English literature, created in him fathomless interest in Western literature, and made him familiar with the European principles of criticism. As a result of his encouragement, Rabindranath rendered a few English poems into Bengali. His earlier works like *Banaphul* were much influenced by his masterpiece *Udashini.* Rabindranath admits his indebtedness to Akshay Chandra in these words:

> A genuine delight in literature is much rarer than erudition, and it was this enjoyment in Akshay Babu which used to awaken my own literary appreciation. He was as liberal in his friendships as in his literary criticisms. Among strangers he was as a fish out of water, but

> among friends discrepancies in wisdom or age made no difference to him. With us boys he was a boy. When he took his leave, late in the evening, from the *mujlis* of our elders, I would buttonhole and drag him to our school - room. There, with undiminished geniality he would make himself the life and soul of our little gathering, seated on the top of our study table. On many such occasions I have listened to him going into a rapturous dissertation on some English poem; engaged him in some appreciative discussion, critical inquiry, or hot dispute; or read to him some of my own writings and been rewarded in return with praise unsparing.[1]

Viharilal, who was a prominent member of the literary circle at Rabindranath's house and who was acknowledged as the creator of a new age of poetry in Bengal, was a constant source of creative inspiration for the young Rabindranath. This literary circle launched a journal named *Bharati* in 1877, and Rabindranath was assigned the work of collecting articles for it. The journal gave him an opportunity to write both poetry and prose, and thus came out from his pen literary pieces like *Banaphul, Kavilkahini, Bhanu Singha Padavali, Bhikharini, Karuna,* a critical article on *Meghnadvadh,* etc. The influence of Viharilal is clearly perceptible on his musical play, *Valmiki Pratibha.* The Tagore family was as much given to literature as to music, and hence Rabindranath developed a unique taste for music early in life.

The medieval Vaishnava poetry influenced Tagore right from the beginning of his literary career. The most notable work of his teens, *Bhanu Singha Padavali,* fully bears a testimony to it. The impact of the medieval Vaishnava poets on him is explicit in his use of language and imagery. He did not hesitate in naming himself a medieval Vaishnava poet, Bhanu Singha, and in using Brajabuli dialect in which Vidyapati, the renowned Vaishanava poet of the fourteenth century, wrote much of his great poetry. Te impact of the Vaishnava poets on him is further visible in his ceaseless treatment of the theme of unfathomable love of Radha and Krishna About the profound influence of the old Vaishnava poetry on him, Rabindranath avers:

> As I have said I was a keen student of the series of old Vaishnava poems which were being collected and published by Babus Akshay Sarkar and Saroda Mitter. Their language, largely mixed with Maithili, I found difficult to understand; but for that very reason I took all the more pains to get at their meaning. My feeling towards them was that same eager curiosity with which I regarded the ungerminated sprout within the seed, or the undiscovered mystery under the dust-covering of the earth. My enthusiasm was kept up with the hope of bringing to light some unknown poetical gems, as I went deeper and deeper into the unexplored darkness of this treasure-house.[2]

The impact of the Vaishnava poetry on Tagore will be examined, in detail later on in chapter III of the present dissertation.

Rabindranath was greatly influenced by the religious and social reforms brought about by Raja Rammohan Roy and Maharshi Devendranath, as well as by the cultural nationalism pleaded by Bankim Chandra Chattopadhyaya in his works. The clash between Hinduism and Islam was replaced by the conflict between Hinduism and Christianity in the second half of the nineteenth century. Hindu students were being converted into Christians by the Mission Schools. What was shocking for the Hindus was the conversion of Michael Madhusudan Dutt and of the family of Toru Dutt into Christians. Brahmo Society, founded by Raja Rammohan Roy and revitalized by Maharshi Devendranath and other intellectuals like Akshay Kumar Dutta, worked vigorously against this unhappy and unfortunate trend in Bengali society. Rabindranath, naturally, became the champion of Hinduism and the healthy social and religious reforms already initiated by his illustrious predecessors and contemporaries. Bankim Chandra's patriotic zeal also fired his imagination, with the result young Rabindranath became very fond of patriotic poems. No wonder cultural pride and patriotism formed the core of many of his later literary masterpiece.

Rabindranath Tagore's visits to Europe ever since his childhood deeply impresend him, widening the horizons of his comprehension of life and art. During his stay in England, he read English literature under the guidance of Professor Henry Morley whose lectures on *Antony* and *Cleopatra, Coriolanus* and *Religio Medici* left an indelible imprint on his tender, sensitive mind. He happened to go through the works of Shelley, Byron, Keats, Browning and Swinburne, and translated a few poems of Shelley into Bengali. However, it was European music and dances that fascinated him more than literature in his young age. Nevertheless, at the age of eighteen only he could publish in the *Bharati* essays on Petrarch and Laura, the Saxons and Anglo-Saxon literature, the Normans and Anglo-Norman literature, Dante, Goethe and Chatterton. His stay in England for about fourteen months brought him in close contact with Loken Palit, a young Indian boy, living in England for the purpose of taking up I.C.S. Under the influence of his young learned friend, Rabindranath developed a liberal view of art and the belief in literature for its own sake, rejecting the earlier notion that art was essentially a means of expressing traditional thoughts, religious beliefs, etc. His intimacy with Loken also created in him on unshakable interest in comparative literature. Acknowledging his indebtedness to Loken, Rabindranath writes in *Reminiscences*:

> Loken's boisterous delight in literature was as the wind in the sails of my literary adventure. And when at the height of my youth I was driving the tandem of prose and poetry at a furious rate, Loken's unstinated appreciation kept my energies from flagging for a moment. Many an extraordinary prose or poetical flight have I taken in his bungalow in the mofussil. On many an occasion did our

> literary and musical gatherings assemble under the auspices of the evening star, to disperse, as did the lamplights at the breezes of dawn, under the mornings star.[3]

During this period when Shakespeare, Milton and Byron were his literary gods, he composed many poems, the most significant of which was "*Bhagna Hridaya*" (Broken Heart"). When he returned from England, he found Indian Renascence swaying over the entire Bengal. Under the new sky, he formulated new principles of art and literature reflected in the creative works he published during those years. Haunted by Thomas Moore's Irish Melodies and other Western literary standards, and at the same time taking the best of the Indian literary traditions, he brought out a musical drama, *Valmiki Pratibha*, inevitably presenting a happy blending of the European and Indian Tunes. It was followed by two more musical plays, *Kal Mrigaya* and *Mayar Khela*, and by a collection of poems entitled *Heart-Wilderness*. The poems contained in the collection were primarily the result of contemplation, having little to do with the external life and worldly reality. Commenting on these poems, he remarks:

> Much of what I wrote, when thus my life had no commerce with the outside, when I was engrossed in the contemplation of my own heart, when my imaginings wandered in many a disguise amidst causeless emotions and aimless longings, has been left out of that edition; only a few of the poems originally published in the volume entitled *Evening Sons* finding a place there, in the Heart-Wilderness group.[4]

The encouragement and admiration that his early works received from the literary luminaries of his time infused him with new creative vigour and inspiration. It was a matter of pride and rare distinction for him to see Bankim Chandra Chatterji and Babu Priyanath Sen, who was a distinguished scholar of several literatures of the world and whose literary judgements he valued very much, appreciating his works publicly. Bankim Chandra Chatterji's vociferous admiration of his *Evening Songs* meant much to him, and he records it in the following words:

> When the *Evening Songs* first saw the light they were not hailed with any flourish of trumpets, but none the less they did not lack admirers. I have elsewhere told the story of hcw, at the wedding of Mr. Ramesh Chandra Dutt's eldest daughter, Bankim Babu was at the door, and the host was welcoming him with the customary garland of flowers. As I came up Bankim Babu eagerly took the garland, and placing it round my neck, said: "The wreath to him, Ramesh; have you not read his Evening Songs?" And when Mr. Dutt avowed he had not yet done so, the manner in which Bankim Babu expressed his opinion of some of them amply regarded me.[5]

Early in his manhood, Rabindranath had a unique experience, an epiphany, a great moment of illumination or profound insight or radiance which he called "a momentous revolution within him." It deeply influenced his whole being as well as his creative writings. This happened when he was staying with his brother Jyotirindra at a house in Calcutta on Sudder Street near the Museum. The profound realisation dawned upon him suddenly one evening and one morning separately, shaking wildly his entire self and revealing to him beneath the surface triviality of the world the immensity of joy and beauty. A propos of this, he affirms:

> One day, late in the afternoon, I was pacing the terrace of our Jorasanko house. The after-glow of the sunset combined with the wan twilight in a way which scemed to give the approaching evening a specially wonderful attractiveness for me. Even the walls of the adjoining house seemed to grow beautiful. Is this uplifting of the cover of triviality from the everyday world, I wondered, due to some magic in the evening light? Never!
>
> I could see at once that it was the effect of the evening which had come within *me*; its shades had obliterated my *self*. While the self was rampant during the glare of day,

> everything I perceived was mingled with and hidden by it. Now that the self was put into the background, I could see the world in its own true aspect. And that aspect has nothing of triviality in it, it is full of beauty and joy.
>
> Since this experience I repeatedly tried the effect of deliberately suppressing my *self* and viewing the world as a mere spectator, and was invariably rewarded with a sense of special pleasure. I remember I tried also to explain to a relative how to see the world in its true light, and the incidental lightening of one's own sense of burden which follows such vision; but, as I believe, with no success.
>
> Then I gained a further insight which has lasted all my life.
>
> The end of Sudder Street, and the trees on the Free School grounds opposite, were visible from our Sudder Street house. One morning I happened to be standing on the verandah looking that way. The sun was just rising through the leafy tops of those trees. As I continued to gaze, all of a sudden a covering seemed to fall away from my eyes, and I found the world bathed in a wonderful radiance, with waves of beauty and joy swelling on every side. This radiance pierced in a moment through the folds of sadness and despondency which had accumulated over my heart, and flooded it with this universal light.[6]

This unique experience gave birth to an exquisite poem entitled *"The Awakening of the Waterfall"*, and threw Rabindranath into a state of self-forgetful bliss for sometime. He described this period of his life in the following two poetic lines:

> I know not how of a sudden my heart flung open its doors,
>
> And let the crowd of worlds rush in, greeting each other—[7]

A few days later on the Darjeeling hills he composed the lyric, *"The Echo"*, which formed the last piece of the collection *Morning Songs*. In "Echo", the poet reveals, by way of a parable, the realisation that the True, the Good, is the stream flowing from the Infinite towards the finite, and that Beauty and Joy are the echo of this flowing stream returning towards the Infinite. Explaining the unforgettable vision and the comprehension of the mastery of the external and internal life, of artistic creation, and of the universe which were partly reflected in the lyric "The Echo" and which formed the very core of his great artistic creations, Tagore states:

> When from the original fount in the depths of the Universe streams of melody are sent forth abroad, their echo is reflected into our heart from the faces of our beloved and the other beauteous things around us. It must be, as I suggested, this Echo which we love, and not the things themselves from which it happens to be reflected; for that which one day we scarce deign to glance at may be, on another, the very thing which claims our whole devotion.
>
> I had so long viewed the world with external vision only, and so had been unable to see its universal aspect of joy. When of a sudden, from some innermost depth of my being, a ray of light found its way out, it spread over and illuminated for me the whole universe, which then no longer appeared like heaps of things and happenings, but was disclosed to my sight as one whole. This experience seemed to tell me of the stream of melody issuing from the very heart of the universe and spreading over space and time, re-echoing thence as waves of joy which flow right back to the source.
>
> When the artist sends his song forth from the depths of a full heart that is joy indeed. And the joy is redoubled when this same song is wafted back to him as hearer. If, when the creation of the Arch-Poet is thus returning back to him in a flood of joy, we allow it to flow over our consciousness, we at once, immediately, become aware, in an inexpressible manner, of the end to which this flood is streaming. And as we become aware our love goes

> forth; and our *selves* are moved from their moorings and would fain float down the stream of joy to its infinite goal. This is the meaning of the longing which stirs within us at the sight of Beauty.
>
> The stream which comes from the Infinite and flows toward the finite—that is the True, the Good; it is subject to laws, definite in form. Its echo which returns towards the Infinite is Beauty and Joy which are difficult to touch or grasp, and so make us beside ourselves. This is what I tried to say by way of a parable or a song in *The Echo*. That the result was not clear is not to be wondered at, for neither was the attempt then clear unto itself.[8]

Tagore's marriage with eleven year old Mrinalini Devi on December 9, 1883 lent a new impetus to his creative urge, with the result he brought out a large number of poems, short stories, essays, etc. In fact, this period of his life that he spent at Shelidah with his wife was by far the most creative and rewarding period of his life. The partition of Bengal in 1905 filled him with great patriotic zeal, resulting in a good number of patriotic writings of high order. His visit to Ghazipur in U.P. during this period proved very fruitful in that he wrote most of the poems of *Manasi* there. He established a school named santiniketan at Bolpur in 1901 with the specific aim of making it a cultural centre after the model of *Gurukulas*. This school developed in 1920 into a university called *Visva-Bharati*, upholding the lofty ideal of uniting humanity by fostering in people understanding, love and truth.

Five successive deaths in the family from 1902 onwards—viz. the death of his wife in 1902, of his daughter Renuka in 1903, of his dear pupil Satish Roy in 1904, of his father in 1905 and of his youngest son in 1907—shook Rabindranath's entire being terribly but gave him a new insight into the mystery of death and life and a profoundly philosophic vision of the universe which found expression in his great works, including his *magnum opus*, *Gitanjali*. Many of the songs of *Gitanjali, Kheya* and *Naivedya* emanated from his mood of renunciation caused by these deaths in the family. The poems collected in the volume entitled *Smaran* (Remembrance) were composed to commemorate the memory of his wife. He expresses his view of death and life, as envisaged by him after witnessing five deaths in the family in quick succession in these words in *Reminiscences*:

> Just as a young plant, surrounded by darkness, stretches itself, as it were on tiptoe, to find its way out into the light, so when death suddenly throws the darkness of negation round the soul it tries and tries to rise into the light of affirmation. And what other sorrow is comparable to the state wherein darkness prevents the finding of a way out of the darkness?
>
> . . . .
>
> . . . .
>
> The all-pervading pressure of worldly existence compensates itself by balancing life against death, and thus it does not crush us. The terrible weight of an unopposed life-force has not to be endured by man—this truth came upon me that day as a sudden, wonderful revelation.
>
> ... Death had given me the correct perspective from which to perceive the world in the fullness of its beauty, and as I saw the picture of the Universe against the background of Death I found it entrancing.[9]

It is this comprehensive vision of the mystery and meaning of life and death which is projected, time and again, in his immortal literature.

World War I with all its disaster and the collapse of values rudely shocked Rabindranath and filled him with a sense of waste and melancholy. However, Mahatma Gandhi, whom he chanced to meet in 1915 for the first time, gave him new hope and vigour. His righteousness and simplicity impressed him deeply. It was Rabindranath who called Gandhiji Mahatma and since then this title has become permanently associated with the greatest man of modern India. Gandhiji must have contributed to the thematic, tonal and linguistic simplicity and moral intensity of his later artistic creations.

NOTES AND REFERENCES

1. Rabindranath Tagore, *Reminiscences* (Delhi: Macmillan Pocket Tagore Edition, 1983), pp. 125-27.
2. *Ibid.*, pp. 136-37.
3. *Ibid.*, pp. pp. 177-78.
4. *Ibid.*, p. 200.
5. *Ibid.*, pp. 213-14.
6. *Ibid.*, pp. 216-17.
7. *Ibid.*, p. 220
8. *Ibid.*, pp. 223-25.
9. *Ibid.*, pp. 258-60.

2

Ancient Indian Influences on Tagore: The '*Vedas*', the '*Upanishads*', etc.

Of all the influences on Rabindranath Tagore, the most conspicuous and consistent is that of the *Vedas*, the *Upanishads*, the *Gita*, etc. Since it is very explicit and all-pervasive in all his writings, creative and expository, it is almost impossible to deal with it, in all details, in just one chapter of a formal work such as this. But a full-length study of the influences on Tagore will surely be incomplete, if this aspect of it is not touched at all. Hence the need for a discussion of it. In fact, the impact of the *Upanishads* and the *Vedas* on Tagore's creative mind cannot be exaggerated, forever since his father, during wanderings at the Himalayas, taught the boy Rabindranath to chant the holy verses of the *Upanishads*, these monumental Hindu scriptures coloured all his thoughts throughout his life. The child Rabindranath very often saw his father reciting the sacred hymns from the *Upanishads* to seek communion with the Eternal. Recalling all this, Tagore records:

> By the time the sun rose, my father, after his prayers, finished with me our morning milk, and then, I standing at his side, he would once more hold communion with

God, chanting the Upanishads.[1]

No wonder Tagore's expository writings — *Sadhana, Personality, Creative Unity, The Religion of Man, Towards Universal Man, Reminiscences, Angel of Surplus, Letters* etc. — are interspersed with countless references to the *Vedas* and the *Upanishads*, and this amply proves that he is soaked in them. His commendable lectures delivered at the Harvard University in 1913 and later on published under the title *Sadhana*, are, as a matter of fact, a poet's interpretation of the *Upanishadic* verses. Ernest Rhys, to whom the book is dedicated, is not far from the truth when he avers: "In Tagore you feel the humanity that was in the Son of Man, comforting the children of light in their awe of the Eternal. In him the spirits of the *Upanishads* reach the same threshold."[2] In this chapter an attempt will be made to bring out the impact of the ancient sacred scriptures on Tagore's ideas on art, God, reality, personality, etc. that run throughout the entire corpus of his works, and form the solid foundation of his great literature.

The *Righis* of ancient India comprehended the truth that the human mind could never fully know the Absolute, the *Brahma*, and in this connection Tagore quotes a line from the *Upanishads*: "I do not think that I know Him, nor that I know Him not." However, the *Rishis* who created the *Upanishads* and the *Vedas* could realise Him, during their sustained contemplations on Him, as Bliss. (*Anandam*), as indivisible Joy, manifesting Itself in Beauty, Love, Light, etc. The entire being of Tagore was fully immersed in this vision of the *Brahma* permeating the cosmos as well as the innermost heart of man, and it is this vision which is the perennial source of all his artistic activities. No wonder like the creators of the *Upanishads*, Tagore could also sing:

> I know the joy that hidden in the heart of Light
> Touches me, is one with my soul.
> I have been annointed in the holy waters of Consciousness,

That flow from the font of Light,
And have my share of immortality.
In this multitudinous earth
I can be united with the supreme Me
And enter the path of Blise.[3]

Tagore endorses the old Indian ideal of joy as the soul of art, and he lucidly exposes the fact that this concept is based on the *Upanishadic* concept of God as creator not out of necessity but simply out of joy in, and love for, creation. In deed, it is for the sake of deep, unique enjoyment that the artist creates a work of art, and it is for the sake of the experience of joy that people care for it. But this enjoyment must have disinterestedness, otherwise a work of art cannot transcend time and space, and cannot become a dear possession of all lovers of art of all times and climes. In fact, the perennial fountain head of art is the artist's experience of the fullness of joy in the act of artistic creation, and not some outer urge or compulsion. In this regard, the artist is like God, who, as stated in the *Upanishads*, it incessantly immersed in creation not out of any necessity, but out of sheer fullness of joy, out of his love for creation which naturally reveals Him. Since the artist objectively projects his artistic idea which embodies his fullness of delight, he achieves a sort of detachment from his artistic idea, and hence is able to explore and communicate it truthfully and comprehensively. Apropos of this, Tagore writes:

> The artist who has a joy in the fullness of his artistic idea objectifies it and thus gains it more fully by holding it afar. It is joy which detaches ourselves from us, and then gives it form in creations of love in order to make it more perfectly our own. Hence there must be this separation, not a separation of repulsion but a separation of love.[4]

As a very intense sense of joy emanates from the experience of love, the latter forms the core of the large corpus of artistic works in the world. According to the ancient Indian metaphysics, man feels at the bottom of his being that he is separated from his own self, and craves for a re-union. It is because of this unfathomable feeling that he thinks that it is only through love that he can achieve the union which is final. Consequently, love becomes a great impulse in man bringing forth all his best creative activities. This kind of love is not simply an impulse in man, urging him to express himself in artistic creations, but it comprises truth which is law also.[5] Accentuating love as the sure source of delight and hence the very essence of the creative spirit permeating the universe and art, Tagore maintains:

> . . . whatever name our logic may give to the truth of human unity, the fact can never be ignored that we have our greatest delight when we realise ourselves in others, and this is the definition of love.[6]

Tagore repeatedly avers that it is boundless joy which finds expression in all artistic activities, whatsoever form they may take. "The joy, which is without form, must create, must translate itself into forms."[7] Thus the singer expresses his joy in the form of a song, the poet in the form of a poem, and so on and so forth. In a word, "Man in his role of a creator is ever creating forms, and they come out of his abounding joy."[8] This fathomless joy which is behind every creation and sustains everything, is not something very rare; it is quite common because, as Tagore affirms, "Beauty is omini present, therefore everything is capable of giving us joy."[9]

Patently, Tagore pins his faith in the Indian concept of creation as propounded in the *Upanishads*, according to which infinite joy is the essence of all creative activities, including the artistic ones. The artist strives to express faithfully whatever he truly thinks, feels and realises. He perceives all this happening in him under the compulsion of some force which works not only in him but in the entire universe. This force, which permeates the universe and hence the individual artist also, acts according to its own nature and beyond the control of an individual, howsoever gifted he may be. What is remarkable about this force is that it overflows the artist with joy the moment he submits himself to it. It is in this state that he easily gives true and full expression to whatever he genuinely things and feels. This spirit of joy, governing the entire cosmos, works in the artist and enables him to accomplish a work of art saturated with delight. In support of his assertion, Tagore quotes from the *Upanishads*:

> For of Joy are born all created things.[10]

Just as children, steeped in pure joy, have the power of creating their world of beauty and delight out of every trivial thing, so the artist does.

Joy is the very breath of art yet in another way. Through the process of continuous growth, man has come to identify himself with the world, if not with the whole of it, at least with some significant parts of it. Naturally, man finds joy in all that with which he feels united. Art, in Tagore's opinion, is man's expression of joy stemming from the realisation of this unity or identification. Man's physical, chemical and biological self, as well as his personal self, strive for fulfilment by living in harmony with the variegated parts of the external world and with other human beings. Elucidating the point, Tagore asserts:

> In art we express the delight of this unity by which this world is realized as humanly significant to us. I have my physical, chemical and biological self; my knowledge of it extends through the extension of my knowledge of the physical, chemical and biological world. I have my personal self, which has its communication with our feelings, sentiments and imagination, which lends itself to be coloured by our desires and shaped by our imageries.[11]

Inevitably, art aims at embodying, and transmitting to others, joy arising out of the artist's awareness of the union of the within and the without. This union can be achieved either through the pressure of need or through the emotional being. When confined to the world of need alone, the union has its impact only on the surface of our life. On the other hand, the emotional union of the within and the without imparts man great joy by making our consciousness richer and by widening our individuality, for it is very profound and vast in its nature and scope, Hence Tagore's conclusion: "Art and Literature have for their object this greater joy of profound union and self-enlargement."[12]

In support of his view of joy as the soul of art because all the physical object of the cosmos, howsoever humble or lofty they may be, embody the Eternal Joy of the Infinite, Tagore quotes the *Upanishads*: "All appearances, from the speck of dust at our feet to the far away stars in the galaxy, are manifestation of His Immortal Delight, *anandarupamamritam yadvibhati*."[13] This "Immortal Delight' is the ultimate Truth and Beauty as the ancient Indian *Rishis* have repeatedly pointed out, and every great work of art is primarily concerned with It. Apropos of this, Tagore states:

> Art and literature being another evidence or view of things—that the Truth is Joy. Together they but annotate what the sages have always known that we live, move and have our being in the Immortal Delight, which is Truth in its aspect of Beauty.[14]

Tagore derives his idea of the amalgam of the infinite and the finite from the *Upanishads* wherein it is reiterated that it is necessary for man to acquire the knowledge of both the finite and the infinite, for the former helps him to go beyond death and the latter enables him to attain immortality. This leads him to infer that man's (particularly the artist's) personality is not merely individual, but also universal, and a true work of art embodies such a personality in which the individual and the infinite become one. If the knowledge of the finite lacks in the essence of the universe, though it is something concrete, the absolute infinite without the touch of the finite is merely emptiness, leading man to a deeper darkness. This is the reason why the Eternal combines the finite and the infinite, and the artist also does the same. Accentuating the absolute necessity of the fusion of the infinite and the finite, Tagore writes:

> Therefore Ishopanishad in the following verse says:
>
> 'He who knows that the knowledge of the finite and the infinite is combined in one, crosses death by the help of the knowledge of the finite and achieves immortality by the help of the knowledge of the infinite.'
>
> The infinite and the finite are one as song and singing are one. The singing is incomplete; by a continual process of death it gives up the song which is complete. The absolute infinite is like a music which is devoid of all definite tunes and therefore meaningless.
>
> The absolute eternal is timelessness, and that has no meaning at all, -- it is merely a word. The reality of the eternal is there, where it contains all times in itself.
>
> Therefore Upanishad says:' They enter the region of darkness who pursue the transitory. But they enter the region of still greater darkness who pursue the eternal. He who knows the transitory and the eternal combined together crosses the steps of death by the help of the transitory and reaches immortality by the help of the eternal.'[15]

Tagore's belief that great art deals with the relationship existing between the Infinte Being and the finite self of man is founded on his study and understanding of the *Vedas* and the *Upanishads*. No wonder her refers to the *Upanishad* which explains this relationship with the help of the parable of two birds sitting on the same bough, one of which feeds while the other only looks on. Tagore points out that both the birds exist in man, the objective one absorbed in life's business and the subjective one immersed in the detached delight of vision. The joy of vision is greater than anything else, and the artist is primarily concerned with it. Art embodies man's recognition of a reality, an illumination which is much higher and greater than the objective reality or the dull happenings of daily life. The realisation of the higher reality illumines the world and enables us to feel it with our soul. That is why, Tagore defines art as "the response of man's creative soul to the call of the Real."[16] Tagore refers to the ancient Indian prayer "Lead us from the unreal to Reality", and believes that this is the aim of art.

Even in some aspects of his concept of beauty in art, Tagore shows his indebtedness to the ancient Indian *Rishis*. He holds that a true artist is, and has to be, an ascetic. The artist, being the lover of beauty, should consider all kinds of indulgence as taboo. Art can be an embodiment of abiding values only when it is the creation of artist saturated with inner strength. "By succumbing to passions and dissipating his energies; says Tagore, "The artist proves himself disloyal to the ideal of beauty."[17] As beauty is born of discipline and control, so the unruly passions only create a world which is not in harmony with the world around us. Man's anger, greed, etc. blur and distort the reality by making the great appear small, and *vice versa*. Thus the insignificant become enormous, while the infinite and significant disappear from our eyes. Tagore says that the majestic flow of a river and 'the wild gurgling' of a whirlpool fully illustrate this difference. Those, who discern and point to thrilling beauty in such phenomena of life and are absorbed in this type of 'revel riot', are certainly far from truth. But great art is concerned with the whole of things and happenings, apprehending and revealing the hidden world of harmony and truth which provide us a highly pleasing and satisfactory experience. No wonder all mature arts possess a classical dignity born of a severity, and do not bother about the surface beauty and details. "To the untrained observer," says Tagore, "all this might look rather bare but for the lover of beauty it yields a richer harvest."[18] Also, Tagore believes that without controlling sensual desires, we can never see and comprehend the purest substance of Beauty. This, according to Tagore, accounts for the Indian sages' stress on the need for discipline and restraint in life, which alone can enable us to pursue beauty in its purest essence, and is not meant to dispel beauty and joy from life.

Under the impact of the holy ancient Indian scriptures, Rabindranath Tagore holds that the essence of all reality is in the Eternal Person, and not in any kind of law, phenomenon or substance. If the universe is not the incarnation of the Supreme Person, it is nothing but a ceaseless fabric and illusion. The artist, like the Supreme Being, has the deathless personality which finds expression in all his deeds. In support of his assertion, Tagore refers to the poet of *Isha Upanishad* and puts his ideas on the subject in these words:

> From the dawn of our history the poets and artists have been infusing the colours and music of their soul into the structure of existence. And from this I have known certainly that the earth and the sky are woven with the fibres of man's mind, which is the universal mind at the same time. If this were not true, then poetry would be false and music a delusion, and the mute world would compel man's heart into utter silence. The Great Master plays; the breath is his own, but the instrument is our mind through which he brings out his songs of creation, and therefore I know that I am not a mere stranger resting in the wayside inn of this earth on my voyage of existence, but I live is a world whose life is bound up with mine. The poet has known that the reality of this world is personal...[19]

In his concept of the surplus in man, which is behind all his activities, including works of art, Tagore is influenced by an exquisite verse in the *Atharva Veda* which he renders into English as follows: "Righteousness, truth, great endeavours, empire, religion, enterprise, heroism and prosperity, the past and the future, dwell in the surpassing strength of the surplus."[20] Art, religion and all other remarkable thoughts and activities of man are the outcome of the surplus he carries around his personality. This surplus is "like the atmosphere of the earth, bringing to her a constant circulation of light and life and delightfulness."[21] Even architecture, one of the crudest of fine arts, springs from the spirit of surplus in man. Thus a man builds a house for bigger and far more permanent than his physical being. Inevitably, which doing so, he-engrossed in his creative work—feels in his mind the sense of the Eternal. "And this background of the boundless surplus of time," asserts Tagore, "encourages architecture, which seeks a universal value overcoming the miserliness of the present need."[22] Man is gifted with imagination which makes him deeply aware of a higher and greater life, besides that of simple biological and physical needs: it "works at the surplus, and extending beyond the reservation plots of our daily life, builds there the guest chambers of priceless value to offer hospitality to the world-spirit of Man."[23]

Tagore discerns in the old Sanskrit texts the confirmation of his theory that art is the result of the surplus of emotional experience, and cannot be merely confined to social values, moral judgements or intellectual purposes. Man is capable of transcending himself and his surroundings, and this he embodies in works of art. Tagore quotes the remark of Sayanacharya, the famous Vedic commentator: "The food offering which is left over after the completion of sacrificial rites is praised because it is symbolical of Brahma, the original source of the universe."[24] Tagore points out that the remark tresses the fact that *Brahma* is limitless in his superfluity which finds its expression in the eternal process of the world and in all things in life if observed closely. Obviously, Tagore finds the confirmation of this concept of art even in ordinary day-to-day life; the music on the occasion of a festival, the flowers in a vase, and the gaudy colours of a child's dress clearly show the superfluous beyond man's immediate need. Thus the all-pervasive atmosphere of superfluity in life engage man's attention, and art owes its existence to it.

Tagore's belief in the teachings of the *Upanishads* make him evolve the concept that the creative artist owes a lot to the Eternal Being, and hence has responsibility towards Him. For the creative urge and activity of the artist is as much his as of Him. As a matter of fact, it is the Creative Mind that shapes the universe and the world of the artist to give vent to Its Eternal Idea. Thus the artist in his creative moments finds himself a person in whom the Creative Mind has one of Its special centres of an intimate relationship developing into "a deepening consciousness."[25] During this process, the artist is immersed in creative activities which enable him to transcend his "own personal bounds like stars which in their individual fire-bursts are lighting the history of the universe."[26] The artist is filled with a unique joy by realising the meeting of the Creative Mind and his creative instinct, leading to a highly fruitful creative companionship. Tagore himself had this realisation in which he had discerned his religion," the religion of Man, in which the infinite became defined in humanity and came close to me so as to need my love and co-operation."[27] Tagore points out that this idea about artistic creation was expressed in some of his poems addressed to what he labelled *Jivan Devata*, the Lord of his life. A few lines of one of his poems are quoted below to illustrate the point:

> Thou who art the innermost Spirit of my being,
> art thou pleased,
> Lord of my Life?
>
> . . . .
>
> . . . .

> *I wove with the rhythm of colours and songs the cover for thy bed,*
> and with the molten gold of my desires
> I fashioned playthings for thy passing hours.
>
> I know not why thou chosest me for thy partner,
> Lord of my life:
>
> Didst thou store my days and nights,
> *my deeds and dreams for the alchemy of thy art, and string in the chain of thy music my songs of autumn and spring,*
> and gather the flowers from my mature moments for thy crown?[28]

The moment, revealing to the artist his vision, is excessively precious to him, as it enables him to grasp a larger meaning of his own self when the dam between him and what is beyond him vanishes.

Again, it is as a result of his obsession with the ideas of the *Upanishads* that Tagore proclaims evanescent moments, or moments of spiritual realisation as the basic subject of art and literature. Human soul has fathomless craving for the instant realisation of the Infinite Being that also leads her to know herself. That which satisfies this hunger—love or some vision—forms the core of art. Such a realisation over-flows man's entire being with joy, dispelling all fears and drossy desires. And since this realisation or experience is immeasurable, it is indefinable because anything that cannot be measured cannot be defined. Speaking of the nature of the subject-matter of art, Tagore says:

> The Upanishad says of the infinite Being that we can reach Him not with speech, nor with the mind, but by our consciousness of delight, where-with all fear departs from us. Our soul has her hunger for this immediateness of realisation, whereby she is enabled also to know herself.
>
> *The love, the contemplation, the vision that alone can satisfy this hunger finds its place in Literature, in Art.*[29]

Further, under the impact of the ancient Indian scriptures, Tagore points out that the material for artistic creation is supplied by history and society, but the artist uses them without being bound to, and steeped in, them. Hence the historical and social facts cannot explain fully any work of art. The artist usually is not immersed in the common social and political situations; he is a detached being with a lonely soul. In his artistic creations, he discovers and experiences the principle of joy in all things and conveys it to others. This intention of the artist and its accomplishment can transform even historical events into great, universal truths—fit subject for great works of art. Apropos of this, Tagore observes:

> Away with your history, I say. At the helm of creation sits the solitary soul, and it is this that absorbs the various sights and sounds of the world. Through the effort at creation it not only finds but also communicates the principle of delight in all things. All of life's history or events h not been and obviously cannot be told. But this is no great loss, since much of this history is not in any way essential. It is only because of the self-expressive urge of man the creator that history has been dynamic throughout the ages. Let that alone matter, that history which guided by the creative spirit of man moves towards the Vast and the True—beyond history, towards the still centre. The Upanishads knew this truth, and the message that I have derived from them is my own. It is of my making, hence a creation.[30]

To reject Plato's outright condemnation of poetry, Tagore seeks support in the old Indian tradition of the alliance between art and philosophy. He cites the Indian view, according to which the aim of philosophy is to deal with people's life, and not the seclusion of scholarship, and art "falls within the scope of a philosopher, when his reason is illumined into a vision"[31] This is the reason why the great Sankaracharya, a metaphysician whom Plato would not have banished from his Utopia, composed numerous verses of considerable beauty. Likewise, the *Mahabharata* and the *Ramayana* are not only great works of art, but also extremely rich in philosophical speculations. Again, innumerable Indian saints composed and sang verses which glowed with the fire of imagination and the depth of philosophy, dealing with the fundamental question—the meaning of existence. This is particularly true of the Vedic *Rishis*.

Apparently, in India philosophy and art have rightly walked hand in gloves. This has been possible because the two have identical object. Philosophy aims at leading people to the practical path of attaining life's fulfilment which consists of "freedom in truth."[32] Like philosophy, art has the same object before it—viz. the attainment of reality through freedom of mind: "To give us the taste of reality through freedom of mind is the nature of all arts"[33]

Tagore affirms that abstract philosophical thoughts are an integral part of art, for they are inseparably fused into "the fibres of our personal nature,"[34] and this is particularly true of Indian art. To the Indian artist, any particular idea of life has not been simply a logical deduction, but something as real as the air to the bird. He considers it an absolutely essential aspect of the infinite. This is the reason why an idea of life, which is merely an abstraction to one who has a limited sense of reality, becomes an illuminating reality for another who has a vast range of sensibility. This also explains why the Indian mind has been termed as metaphysical by the Western critics -it is metaphysical because it is easily capable of soaring into the realm of the infinite. What is remarkable about India is that to her the infinite is not merely a philosophical abstract, but a reality very much like the sunlight; she sees it, feels it and makes use of it in day-to-day life. No wonder the infinite is so abundantly present in Indian art. To the Indian mind, the universal presence of the infinite is as much a reality as the earth under the feet of a man.

Inevitably, Indian art is strickingly and mainly religious because of the simple fact that God to the Indian is not a distant reality, but an essential aspect of homes and temples. The Indians feel His nearness in all the human relationships of love and affection and in all the festivities in which they so frequently participate. God is present in flowers, fruits, seasons and all the objects of man's worship. He is present in woman who is good, in man who is true, in children, in love songs, and in all the festivities and ceremonies. Indian art and literature, being inseparably related to the Infinite Reality, endeavour to reveal the depth of the mystery pervading the universe and make it human and living. No wonder Tagore asserts: "My religious life and my poetical life have followed the same mysterious line of growth. Somehow they are wedded to each other."[35]

Thus, for Tagore, art and religion spring from one and the same source: both stem from the unknown, mysterious inspiration. In this attitude towards art and religion, Tagore follows the great Indian tradition of saint-poets, for whom religion and art were inalienable from each other, and were merged into one because the two emanated from the same source. This kind of concept of art is not commonly seen in the twentieth century Indian and European artists. It is this fusion of the deep religious zeal and the artistic urge that makes a creative genius produce something really thrilling and captivating. Such an artist comes close to God, the greatest creative artist, about whose wonderful artistic power and impact Tagore writes as follows:

> I know not how thou singest, my master!
>
> I ever listen in silent amazement.
>
> The light of thy music illumines the world. The life breath of thy music runs from sky to sky. The holy stream of thy music breaks through all stony obstacles and rushes on.[36]

Besides the sublime songs collected in *Gitanjali*, quite a large number of his poems reflect his unwavering faith in the *Upanishadic* approach to the reality of the Infinite, cosmos, life and death. The *Balaka* poems (*A Flight of Swans*), a volume of forty-five poems only, which constitute a landmark in the development of Tagore the creative artist, evince the poet's absorption in the philosophy of the *Vedas*. The essence of these poems is that stagnation means death, while continuous change and movement stand for life. The following lines evidence it:

> As long as I am stagnant,
> I gather great wealth,
> And never sleep,
> Like an insect I gnaw the earth,
> Heavier grows the weight of sorrow,
> Life, with its cautious brain and chill of doubt. Grows white with age...
> Purified from that bath of Movement.
> I come,
> And drinking its ambrosia,
> Youth blooms constantly new.[37]

The poet exposes the Indian belief that life as a continuous movement has before it the ultimate goal of building a bridge between the finite self and the Infinite. Inevitably, the human soul is engrossed in ceaseless efforts to seek and meet the Eternal. Apropos of this, the poet writes:

> O homeless wanderer,
> The soundless melody resounds in your march.
> Do you hear the Infinite Beyond incessantly?
> Her love is terrible,
> Therefore you are homeless.[38]

Thus, the finite self, according to the teachings of the *Upanishads,* through innumerable failures, sufferings and death, at last attains God, who is Bliss and the Ultimate Glory that shines beyond death. Tagore puts this poetically in these words:

> The travail of the night,
> Will it not usher in the dawn?

In the night of sorrow, under death's blow,
When Man bursts his mortal bounds,
Will not God stand revealed
In his Glory?[39]

An exquisite long poem named "Tapobhanga" (Breaking of Penance"), which does not form a part of any of the major well-known collections of Tagore's poems, is analysed here briefly to show how Tagore's mind and art were soaked in Vedic philosophy and culture. It is a well-established fact that in ancient age no other civilisation could cultivate true spiritualism like that of the Vedic civilisation, which focussed all its energy on the comprehension of the nature of the Great Unknown and His manifested powers. Unlike the ancient Greeks and the Romans, the Vedic sages did not recognise many Gods. The *Vedas* speak of the reality of One True God, of other separate existences as only His manifestations, and of the concentrated manifestation of His power as *Shakti*. The poem, "Tapobhanga", is abut the Supreme Lord of the *Vedas*, described in one of the hymns of the *Upanishads* as *Siva* who with his consort *Uma* (His Power, *Shakti*) practises according to the Indian scriptures, penance and *Yoga*, as is customary with Him, on the high peaks of mount *Kailash*. Regarding this concept of *Siva*, the poet must have been inspired by the Sanskrit poet Kalidasa who has portrayed Lord Siva gloriously in his writings which Tagore read with admiration on his own confession. But the primary source of this great poem as the *Vedas*, for "the poet's mind," as Rabindra Nath Choudhary rightly remarks, "was saturated with the conception of the *Upanishadas* underlining the unity of God who has been variously described in the *Upanishadas* (end part of the Vedas). In one such ode to the Lord he was described as *Siva*."[40]

The poem is undoubtedly addressed to the Supreme Lord of the *Vedas*, though the poet also uses the make-up of the Siva, the Lord of *Uma*, to adore the image of the Supreme Lord who may have numberless devotees. There may be innumerable individual souls having love and devotion for the Eternal Soul, the Supreme Lord. In the following lines, cited from the poem, the poet addresses to the One True God of the *Vedas*, also called *Siva*:

> You are the cowherd of eternal time your horn
> blows in the dusk;
> The days, your bovine-charge, return back to
> your still fold
> With anxious hasty steps.[41]

Again, at the very beginning of the second line of the poem, He is addressed as "Lord of endless time". This Infinite is also Joy, Good and Beauty. Thus the poet, addressing Him, says:

> You yourself found out your profound beauty.
> Joyously you held out in your hand the lustrous
> vessel of nectar
> For the hunger of the universe.
>
> . . . .
>
> . . . .
>
> I glimpsed the radiance of smile inlaid in comeliness
> I saw the hesitant gesture of joy of the
> blushing one—
> The ripples of beauty.[42]

Most of the songs of *Gitanjali* have an indelible stamp of the profound thoughts and beliefs for which the *Vedas* and the *Upanishads* are admired with astonishment all over the World. No wonder Edward J. Thompson observes: "what is best in *Gitanjali* is an anthology from the ages of Indian thought and brooding."[43] This is the reason why it is not difficult for an Indian to analyse many of these lyrics from this angle. In support of this assertion, a few of them are discussed here.

The very first lyric is written with a spirit of humility and adoration of the Infinite, who is present in all the created things. The line, "This frail vessel thou emptiest again and again, and fillest it ever with fresh life", refers to the theory of reincarnation of souls after death as propounded in our ancient holy texts, and it echoes the though of the *Gita* (II,22). Lyric XXX points out that it is very difficult to escape from one's ego that accompanies one invariably everywhere and every time. This is *Vedantic* belief that the basic cause of everything that binds man is ego which can not be got rid of without deep meditation. Lyrics LVII and LVIII are the poetic reproduction of the ancient sages' belief that God is Light and Joy that permeate the entire universe. Like the Vedic *Rishis,* Tagore in Song LXIII expresses his unflinching belief in the omnipresence of God Who is the only true companion and saviour of human soul everywhere in this world as well as in others. To quote his own words:

> Through birth and death, in this world or in others, wherever thou leadest me it is thou, the same, the one companion of my endless life whoever linkest my heart with bonds of joy to the unfamiliar.[44]

In song LXV Tagore paints God as poet's poet whose expression and joy are the fountain-head of all the musical poetic compositions of all other poets. This is a lyrical exposition of the *Upanishadic* idea of God as the primeval poet: *'kavirmnishi paribhuh swayambhu."*

Song LXIX is a spontaneous, poetic expression of one of the basic ancient Indian thoughts that human soul or life is an integral part of the Everlasting Who manifests Himself in all the objects of the world, overflowing them with his all-pervasive Joy. The following lines of this song put Tagore beside the great Indian *Rishis*:

> The same streams of life that runs through my veins night and day runs through the world and dances in rhythmic measures.

> It is the same life that shoots in joy through the dust of the earth in numberless blades of grass and breaks into tumultuous waves of leaves and flowers.[45]

Lyric LXXI is about illusion (*maya*) which is repeatedly referred to in most of the old Indian scriptures. According to the Indian saints, God makes man by severing a part of Himself, and thus is created the coloured shadow on His radiance. Not only this, He separates Himself into many, and this world is the place where one is in search of the other. There is a vivid description of *maya* in the *Gita* in chapter IV and XVIII. The next lyric portrays God as an acknowledged impelling force within man, and as One who weaves the web of *maya* the charms of which make every one forgetful of the reality of life, and as the giver of joys and sorrows to man. The most remarkable line of the lyric, "He it is, the innermost one, who awakens my being with his deep hidden touches."[46] is the record of a mystic experience felt by all *Rishis* and described again and again in the *Upanishads*. Lyric LXXV is an echo of a significant philosophical thought contained in *Mundaka Upanishad*. This song points to the belief that everything flows towards God as everything emanates from Him. Thus the rivers flow just to wash His feet, and the flowers sweeten the air only to serve Him. The *Mundaka Upanishad* (II, 1.6) expresses the same idea in these words: "From Him proceed the oceans and all the mountains and the rivers of every kind; from Him also emanate the annual herbs and the juice, by which the inner Self exists encircled by the gross elements."

It may be said that the entire *Gitanjali* is a yearning of the human soul for the love of the Eternal, as well as for death which is, in a way, the fulfilment of this love. It repeats, in its own way, the message of the *Upanishads* that only by knowing Him, the Infinite, that man conquers death and achieves true freedom. *Gitanjali,* the acme of Tagore's artistic achievement, concludes with a salutation to God. Just as the cranes are homesick and fly back long distances to reach their nests, likewise the soul of a *Rishi* or a mystic like Tagore pines for the Eternal Home and continuously strives hard to reach there after its brief earthly existence. Like any of the hymns of the ancient sages, the last song of *Gitanjali* is a prayer to the One Supreme God to whom the poet bows in salutation and submits himself completely with all his senses, mind, creative activities (songs), and life. God is man's eternal home that he can attain only by merging himself into Him in his entirety. Any detailed analysis of this ennobling song will invariably degrade the distilled sublimity and condensed spiritual profundity of it, and hence it is cited below as it is:

> In one salutation to thee, my God, let all my senses spread out and touch this world at thy feet.
>
> Like a rain-could of July hung low with its burden of unshed showers let all my mind bend down at thy door in one salutation to thee.
>
> Let all my songs gather together their diverse strains into a single current and flow to a sea of silence in one salutation to thee.
>
> Like a flock of homesick cranes flying night and day back to their mountain nests let all my life take its voyage to its eternal home in one salutation to thee.[47]

Tagore's last poems, dictated from his sick bed and later published under the title *Wings of Death,* dwell upon the theme that death is not to be feared at all, for the entire universe is Life imbedded in love that cannot be conquered by death, and hence the physical death is only a new birth of the spirit in the cosmos permeated by the Great Unknown. One of the last few poems of Tagore, composed on January 24, 1941, is reproduced below to show the tremendous impact of the ancient Indian holy texts on this great saint-poet, ceaselessly haunted by the quest for the infinite behind the veil of the finite:

Standing on the threshold
Where creation's drama unfolds,
I see in sudden flashes
The realm beyond Darkness,
Where immersed I lay
In consciousness of the Great Being—
Unexpressed is He,
Unperceived, Unknown!
In this dawn
The words of the *Rishis* rise to my mind:
'Oh Sun! remove the veil that covers thy light!
In thy perfect light
May I see my true self.'
The self that at journey's end
Mingles its breath with the air,
And transforms the body to dust—
May he not disguised as truth
Cast a shadow on life's path!

In the playground of this world,
In joy, the suffering,
I have beheld in sudden flashes
The Infinite behind the veil of the finite;
Have comprehended:
The meaning of this birth lay
In that Beauty ineffable,
In that Song inexpressible!
When the drama ends,
I shall leave behind
In this earth's temple—
My salutation,
My worship,
Whose value death cannot grasp.[48]

To conclude, the influence of the ancient Indian holy scriptures on Tagore is immense, and is clearly visible here and there and everywhere in his writings. He admits it time and again, and we end this discussion with his incisive comment on the *Gayatri* which, according to him, is the most popular religious and philosophical prayer among the Indians and which is almost the very core of all the *Vedas*:

> ... the text of our everyday meditation is the *Gayatri*, a verse which is considered to be the epitome of all the Vedas. By its held we try to realise the essential unity of the world with the conscious soul of man; we learn to perceive the unity held together by the one Eternal Spirit, whose power creates the earth, the sky, and the stars, and at the same time irradiates our minds with the light of a consciousness that moves and exists in unbroken continuity with the outer world.[49]

NOTES AND REFERENCES

1. Rabindranath Tagore, *Reminiscences*, p. 94.
2. *Ernest Rhys, Rabindranath Tagore* (London: Macmillan, 1963), p. 6.
3. Rabindranath Tagore, *Wings of Death* (London: John Murray, 1960), p. 80.
4. Rabindranath Tagore, "The Problem of Self", *Sadhana*, (London: Macmillan and Co. Limited, 1946), p. 79.
5. "From Thought Relics", *A Tagore Reader*, ed. Amiya Chakravarty (New York: The Macmillan Company, 1961), pp. 280-81.
6. "The Creative Spirit", *The Religion of Man* (London: George Allen and Unwin Ltd., 1958), p. 49.
7. "Realisation in Love", *Sadhana*, p. 104.
8. *Ibid.*
9. "The Realisation of Beauty", *Sadhana*, p. 138.
10. *Glimpses of Bengal* (Madras: Macmillan Pocket Tagore Edition, 1985), p. 138.
11. "The Artist", *The Religion of Man*, p. 132.

12. "The Philosophy of Literature", *Angel of Surplus*, ed. Sisirkumar Ghose (Calcutta: Visva-Bharati, 1978), p. 76.
13. "Sense of Beauty", *Angel of Surplus*, p. 59.
14. *Ibid.*, p. 60.
15. "The World of Personality", *Personality*, pp. 56-7.
16. 'The Artist", *The Religion of Man*, p. 139.
17. "Sense of Beauty", *Angel of Surplus*, p. 55.
18. *Ibid.*
19. "The World of Personality", *Personality*, pp. 73-4
20. "The Creative Spirit", *The Religion of Man*, p. 44. (Italics Mine)
21. *Ibid.*, p. 45.
22. *Ibid.*, p. 46.
23. *Ibid.*, p. 55.
24. "The Religion of the Artist", *A Tagore Reader*, p. 230.
25. "The Vision", *The Religion of Man*, p. 96.
26. *Ibid.*
27. *Ibid.*
28. *Ibid.*, p. 97 (Italics Mine)
29. "The Principle of Literature", *Angel of Surplus* p. 86. (Italics Mine)
30. "Historicity in Literature", *Angel of Surplus*, p. 153.
31. 'The Philosophy of our People,", *Angel of Surplus*.
32. *Ibid.*, p. 128.
33. *Ibid.*, p. 129.
34. "What is Art ?", *Personality* (London: Macmillian Company Limited, 1945), p. 25.
35. "From My Life?" *A Tagore Reader*, p. 86.
36. Rabindranath Tagore, *Gitanjali* (Madras: Macmillan Pocket Tagore Edition, 1987). pp. 2-3.

37. Rabindranath Tagore, A Flight of Swans (London: John Murray, 1955), p. 23.

38. *Ibid.*, p. 8.

39. *Ibid.*, p. 27.

40. "Tapobhanga" ("Breaking of Penance"), *Love Poems of Tagore*, Trans. Rabindra Nath Choudhury (Delhi: Orient Paperbacks, 1983), p. 138.

41. *Ibid.*, p. 148.

42. *Ibid.*, p. 146.

43. Edward J. Thompson, *Rabindranath Tagore: His Life and Work* (Calcutta: Y.M. C.A. Publishing House, 1961), p. 80.

44. *Gitanjali*, p. 42.

45. *Ibid.*, p. 46.

46. *Ibid.*, p. 48.

47. *Ibid.*, pp. 67-8.

48. *Later Poems of Tagore*, trans. Aurobindo Bose (Delhi: Orient Paperbacks, 1984), pp. 132-33.

49. *Sadhana*, pp. 7-8.

3

The Influence of Kabir on Tagore

In addition to the influences discussed in the Preceding chapter, Kabir and the Indian Vaishnava poets of the medieval period indubitably contributed most to the growth of Rabindranath's mind and art. Perhaps Kabir helped him most in developing a unique two-faceted vision -viz., cosmopolitan based on a perfect unity in mankind without having the tinge of religious or racial fanaticism of any kind; and mystical founded on a personal realisation of God and on the direct communion between the human soul and the Eternal. Inevitably, Kabir was absolutely inalienable from his being and writings right from his early boyhood to the end of his life. As has been pointed out earlier in the foregoing chapter, Rabindranath came in contact with Kabir's sagacious and mystical poetry at the early age of eleven when he happened to go to the Golden Temple of Amritsar alongwith his father. There he was enthralled by the recitation of some of the songs of Kabir whose one hundred *dohas* (couplets) are contained in *Guru Granth Sahib,* the most significant religious book of the Sikhs.

Rabindranath was irresistibly drawn to Kabir, a saint poet and a social reformer of the fifteenth century, because he was an untiring, enlightened champion of the unity of mankind, hitting very hard at the varied barriers of caste, creed and race dividing man from man, and thus spreading the poison of ill-will and hatred in society. Every since his early boyhood, Rabindranath was deeply pained to see the country torn as under on account of the Hindu-Muslim split, caste-conflicts among the Hindus and the religious intolerance in regard to the mode of worship, idol-worship, etc. In fact, his principal aims in life and literature, to quote the words of Ernest Rhys, were "the Unions of Nations, the destroying of caste, religious pride, race-hatred and race-prejudice—in a word, the "Making of Man."[1] Rabindranath felt convinced that he would be able to achieve his ideals by following and spreading the message of Kabir embodied in his writings, for the latter was the very incarnation of universal values and unprejudiced view of iife, championing vigorously the essential unity in mankind and discarding all social, religious and racial differences. Thus Rabindranath Tagore was the first intellectual, nationalist and social reformer of the nineteenth century who could notice the relevance and immense value of Kabir for the overall well-being of the country.

True, Kabir had no predecessor so far as the real sincere effort to bring the Hindus and Muslims near each other was concerned. He perceived clearly that the basic cause of the hatred between the two communities lay in the religious differences of their modes of worship. Essentially an iconoclast and an inveterate hater of fanaticism and rituals, he, therefore, relentlessly attached both the communities with a view to eliminating all that was bogus and sham in their religions. The following lines of Kabir, as rendered into English by Tagore, can be cited in support of the above assertion:

> I Do not know what manner of God is mine.
>
> The Mullah cries aloud to Him: and why? Is your Lord deaf? The subtle anklets that ring on the feet of an insect when it moves are heard by Him.
>
> Tell your beads, paint your forehead with the mark of your God, and wear matted locks long and showy: but a deadly weapon is in your heart, and how shall you have God?[2]

Another poetical piece of Kabir, translated by Tagore into English, still more clearly reveals and accentuates the meaninglessness and foolishness of the claims of each of the two religions – Islam and Hindu – with regard to its superiority over the other in matters of rituals and worship of God. To quote Kabir in Tagore's words:

> If God be within the mosque, then to whom does this world belong?
>
> If Ram be within the image which you find upon your pilgrimage, then who is there to know what happens without?
>
> Hari is in the East: Allah is in the West. Look within you heart, for there you will find both Karim and Ram;
>
> All the men and women of the world are His living forms.
>
> Kabir is the child of Allah and of Ram: He is my Guru, He is my Pir.[3]

The extracts, quoted above, alongwith numerous poetical utterances of Kabir, go to prove that he was, perhaps, the greatest champion of the unity of religions – particularly Islam and Hindu – by seeing unfailingly the essential similarity existing in all religions. He sought to bring about a synthesis of the two main religions of his age, and thus a communal harmony in the Indian society. Tagore chanced to live, more or less, in a similar situation of communal disharmony, and tried to serve his country in the best possible manner by eliminating it. Whereas in the age of Kabir, the Muslim rulers, ruling over the Hindus, were responsible for the communal frenzy, Tagore saw the British imperialists creating a wider and wider gulf between the two dominant communities of India for the sake of perpetuating their exploitation of India. No wonder he found in Kabir his ideal, followed him and made him popular in the interest of the nation.

Tagore was immeasurably impressed by Kabir for

another reason too: the latter was not only against the religious falsity and fundamentalism but was also against several social evils prevalent in the Indian social life of his times. He particularly considered caste feelings among the Hindus as a very pernicious evil destroying the very vitals of the society. For the welfare of the country, the unity between the Hindus belonging to different castes was as significant as the unity between the Hindus and the Muslims. This convinced Rabindranath that Kabir was a nationalist to the backbone, and was a very intelligent social reformer. For the benefit of the country, he translated as follows a song of Kabir reproaching and rejecting derisively the division of the society on the basis of caste and creed:

> It is needless to ask of a saint the caste to which he belongs;
>
> For the priest, the warrior, the tradesman, and all the thirty-six castes, alike are seeking for God.
>
> It is but folly to ask what the caste of a saint my be;
>
> The barber has sought God, the washerwoman, and the carpenter—
>
> Even Raidas was a seeker after God.
>
> The Rishi Swapacha was a tanner by caste.
>
> Hindus and Moslems alike have achieved that
>
> End, where remains no mark of distinction.[4]

Thus, Rabindranath laid bare and underlined the relevance of Kabir to India till to-day. As a matter of fact, the religious and social evils, which intended to destroy the very foundation of Indian life in the fifteenth century, were equally dangerous in the age of Tagore as in the present times. Through his poetic utterances, Kabir made a vigorous and valiant attempt to emancipate the Indian society from the evils permeating and rotting it. He tried to convince the people that they must do four things to root out the social evils so as to revitalise society and make human existence happy:

1. Abandon all the religious rituals
2. Have faith in one Invisible God.
3. Reject all communal feelings and prejudices
4. Demolish all caste – discriminations

Since all these social evils were as conspicuous in Tagore's age as in Kabir's and since Tagore was as sincerely a social reformer as his great predecessor, it was but natural for him to feel fascinated and deeply influenced by the great fifteenth century social reformer and saint – that is, Kabir.

It was not only as a religious and social reformer that Kabir influenced Tagore; the mysticism of the former also seized the imagination of the latter. Kabir is universally acknowledge as a mystic par-excellence, as one who could realise in his own being the oneness of soul and God forming one Absolute Reality. He imbibed the spirit of Indian mysticism which is very vast and varied, consisting of several methods and modes. He was familiar with the basic mystical approaches of the various sects known in his age, but as a mystic he was mainly influenced by *Sahajiya Siddhas* and *Nath Yogis*, though he maintained his individuality by believing in formless God, and thus by not accepting the *Nath Yogis' Shiva* as his God. Sri Sankaracharya's *Vedanta*, particularly his belief in monism based on the doctrine of the Upanishads,' also contributed much to the mystical vision of Kabir. Obviously, for him, human soul and the soul of *Brahma*, the Eternal Soul, are one and the same. The Infinite manifests Himself in all the objects of the cosmos, static or dynamic. Kabir expresses this belief poetically, rendered into English by Tagore, as follows:

> He Himself is the tree, the seed, and the germ.
> He Himself is the flower, the fruit, and the shade.
> He Himself is the sun, the light, and the lighted.
> He Himself is Brahma, creature, and Maya.[5]

Sankara's doctrine of Advait also encompasses Mayavad, for he regards the world as an illusion, *Maya*. This aspect of Sankara's philosophy deeply impressed Kabir and he, time and again, called *Maya*, illusion or ignorance as an investerate cheat (Thagini). Also, he believed in the state of *Moksha* which is inalienable from the non-duality of the individual and the Absolute. The realisation of the Absolute Non-Duality in life can be attained only through love that brings the individual close to the Absolute. Kabir is correct when he asserts that even after reading books and acquiring immense knowledge through them, one dies and does not really become learned (*Pandit*); the true knowledge and immoratality can be possible only through love. Tagore puts the same thought poetically in *Gitanjali* thus:

> By all means they try to hold me secure who love me in this world. But it is otherwise with thy love which is greater than theirs, and thou keepest me free.[6]

In fact, in Kabir's mysticism we find the harmonious blending of several mystical traditions and strains: the Sufi concept of love, the non-dualistic formless Supreme of the *Vedanta*, the *Vaishnava* sense of devotion, the notion of the Yoga of the *Naths*, etc. In a word, there is hardly any Indian spiritual stream that was not absorbed by him, but at the same time he was quite original in his spiritual and mystical experiences and expressions.

Rabindranath Tagore followed and strengthened the Indian mystical thinking, and was greatly influenced by Kabir in this aspect of his mind and art. However, we can trace the roots of his mysticism in his intuitive awareness of the kinship between his inner being, the Eternal and the world around him that he had had in his early life while staying with his brother in Calcutta. He records it, in detail, in *Reminiscences* and *The Religion of Man*. Apropos of this, he writes in the later work.

> When I was eighteen, a sudden spring breeze of religious experience for the first time came to my life

> and passed away leaving in my memory a direct message of spiritual reality. One day while I stood watching at early dawn the sun sending out its rays from behind the trees, I suddenly felt as if some ancient mist had in a moment lifted from my sight, and the morning light on the face of the world revealed an inner radiance of joy. The invisible screen of the commonplace was removed from all things and all men, and their ultimate significance was intensified in my mind; and this is the definition of beauty. That which was memorable in this experience was its human message, the sudden expansion of my consciousness in the super-personal world of man. The poem I wrote on the first day of my surprise was named 'The Awakening of the Waterfall'. The waterfall, whose spirit lay dormant in its icebound isolation, was touched by the sun and, bursting in a cataract of freedom, it found its finality in an unending sacrifice, in a continual union with the sea. After four days the vision passed away, and the lid hung down upon my inner sight. In the dark, the world one again put on its disguise of the obscurity of an ordinary fact.[7]

Consequently, right from his early days, he would perceive the Eternal in every object, static or dynamic, and could not regard anything or any person as trivial or insignificant because the Supreme Reality or the infinite reflects Himself every where. He was, thus, most deeply concerned with the life within, the inner music that incessantly pervades the entire cosmos.

Like Kabir, Tagore believes that it is only by practising the ideal of love in life that man can realise the eternal or divine love which alone can easily lead him to salvation. It is only love which enables man to attain the state of utter forgetfulness of his restricted salt and the inner unity uniting the whole universe. The great mystics like Kabir and Tagore believe that the true religion of man is the religion of love. Tagore puts his mystical conviction in these lines of *Gitanjali*:

> Yes, I know, this is nothing but thy love, O beloved of my heart—this golden light that dances upon the leaves, these idle clouds sailing across the sky, this passing breeze leaving its coolness upon my forehead.
>
> The morning light has flooded my eyes -this is thy message to my heart. Thy face is bent from above, thy eyes look down on my eyes, and my heart has touched thy feet.[8]

In his humanism also, Tagore was influenced by Kabir. He believes in man as the seeker of truth and the lover of the poor and the neglected. He who works very hard and loves the poor, according to Tagore, is loved by God and can attain Him, and not he who worships loudly in the temple. In this context, the following lyric from *Gitanjali* can be quoted:

> Leave this chanting and singing and telling of beads! Whom dost thou worship in this lonely dark corner of a temple with doors all shut? Open thine eyes and see thy God is not before thee!
>
> He is there where the tiller is tilling the hard ground and where the pathmaker is breaking stones. He is with them in sun and in shower, and his garment is covered with dust. Put off thy holy mantle and even like him come down on the dusty soil!
>
> Deliverance ? Where is this deliverance to be found? Our master himself has joyfully taken upon him the bonds of creation; he is bound with us all for ever.
>
> Come out of thy meditations and leave aside thy flowers and incense ! What harm is there if thy clothes become tattered and stained? Meet him and stand by him in toil and in sweat of thy brow.[9]

In Tagore's concept of God as set forth in his poetry, the echoes of Kabir are clearly felt. Kabir pinned his faith in *nirguna*, formless *Brahma* or God. He, according to him, is ineffable and cannot be described. Of Him it cannot be said definitely that He is within us or without us. Only he who has experienced him knows Him, and he who has not gone through this experience does not have faith in his existence. Kabir asserts:

> O How may I ever express that secret word?
>
> O how can I say He is not like this, and He is like that?
>
> If I say that He is within me, the universe is ashamed:
>
> If I say that He is without me, it is falsehood. He makes the inner and the outer worlds to be indivisibly one;
>
> The conscious and the unconscious, both are His footstools.
>
> He is neither manifest nor hidden, he is neither revealed nor unrevealed:
>
> There are not words to tell that which He is.[10]

Apparently, Kabir is one of those few outstanding mystics of the world who could have a synthetic vision of God. Like Saint Augustine, the Christian mystics and the Sufi poet Jalaluddin Rumi, he has succeeded in resolving the incessant contradictions between the personal and the impersonal, the immanent and the transcendental aspects of the Supreme Being. He accomplishes it by acquiring spiritual intuition which forges unity between these contradictions and presents Him as a perfect whole. To quote Kabir's own expression:

> I shut not my eyes, I close not my ears, I do not mortify my body;
>
> I see with eyes open and smile, and behold His beauty everywhere:
>
> I utter His Name and whatever I see, it reminds me of Him; whatever I do, it becomes His worship.
>
> The rising and the setting are one to me; all contradictions are solved.[11]

Kabir holds that God is not simple abstraction, but is the one Reality. He is both the finite and the infinite and also transcends both. This *Brahma* is the Omnipresent Reality; He is the mind within the mind, the Pure Being beyond both the limitless and the limited. He is the fountain-head of all energy, love and life. The mystic Kabir is bound to overflow with fathomless joy after the realisation of the vision of this Supreme Reality that is within every object, living or non-living, and every object, visible or non-visible, is within It. Speaking of this, he says:

> When He Himself reveals Himself Brahma brings into manifestation That which can never be seen.
>
> As the seed is in the plant, as the shade is in the tree, as the void is in the sky, as infinite forms are in the void—
>
> So from beyond the Infinite, the Infinite comes; and from the Infinite the finite extends.
>
> The creature is in Brahma, and Bahma is in the creature: they are ever distinct, yet every united.
>
> . . . .
>
> . . . .
>
> He Himself is the manifold form, the infinite space;
>
> He is the breath, the word, and the meaning.
>
> He Himself is the limit and the limitless; and beyond both the limited and the limitless is He, the Pure Being.
>
> He is the Immanent Mind in Brahma and in the creature.
>
> The Supreme Soul is seen within the soul,
>
> The Point is seen within the Supreme Soul, And within the Point, the reflection is seen again.
>
> Kabir is blest because he has this supreme vision![12]

Obviously, Kabir's God is beyond any philosophical system, and can be comprehended only through experience. He is *nirguna*, formless, the ultimate one, the Absolute, though the saint poet calls Him by various known names like Hari or Rama by which he never means the son of the king Dashrath.

Like Kabir, Tagore has an unflinching belief in the existence of god with whom Man and Nature are closely associated. But he evinces his faith in both the aspects of God, the transcendent and the immanent. He affirms that the is beyond the human self and the cosmos, and is without the mental or physical attributes, and hence beyond concrete attainment. Nevertheless, he holds that He is the very core of human heart and is not without moral and divine attributes. He is the incarnation of all knowledge and perfection, and is Omnipresent, Omnipotent and Omniscient. At times he addresses Him as a friend, a lover, a companion or a music maker. Like all the mystics of varied faiths and creeds, he believes in God who is "above all, though all and in all". Like Kabir, Tagore's *Brahma* is formless, but He also manifests Himself in the various objects of the visible universe. Though inscrutable without definite form and name, He is felt and realised by man. To quote Tagore's own words:

> In this playhouse of infinite forms I have had my play and here have I caught sight of him that is formless.
>
> My whole body and my limbs have thrilled with his touch who is beyond touch; and if the end comes here, let it come—let this be my parting word.[13]

As Dr. S. Radhakrishnan points out, all the mystics are possessed with contradictions and confusion, and are confronted with "the dilemma of mysticism which makes God sometimes the All, sometimes nothing."[14] To Tagore, God is mainly an all-pervasive presence permeating the cosmos; He illumines the sky, expresses Himself as Joy embodied in the flowers, sky, waves, etc. Thus the contradiction between the transcendent and the immanent aspects of God is only superficial, and not a reality. In fact, the Absolute is the whole universe, and the creation is the play or lila of the Absolute. In the tune and tone of Kabir, Tagore puts his felt mystic experience thus:

> Through birth and death, in this world or in others, wherever thou leadest me it is thou, the same, the one companion of my endess life who ever linkest my heart with bonds of joy to the unfamiliar.
>
> When one knows thee, then alien there is none, then no door is shut. Oh, grant me my prayer that I may never lose the bliss of the touch of the one in the play of the many.[15]

Tagore is closely skin to Kabir in asmuch as he feels the fragrance of spiritual experience coming from within, and not from without. Just as the deer has the perfume (Kasturi) within it but loiters restlessly in search of it, so the God resides within human soul but man frantically strives to discover and attain Him outside his soul. The vision of the Eternal dwelling in man's own soul can be had by him intuitively. Speaking of his realisation of this mystical vision, Tagore says:

> The traveller has to knock at every alien door to come to his own, and one has to wander through all the outer worlds to reach the innermost shrine at the end.
>
> My eyes strayed far and wide before I shut them and said "Here art thou!'
>
> The question and the cry 'Oh, where ?' melt into tears of a thousand streams and deluge the world with the flood of the assurance 'I am !' [16]

Like Kabir, Tagore intends and endeavours to become one with the Everlasting and attain the state of complete union. Like a true mystic, he suffers from a ceaseless quest for Him and an incessant restlessness for achieving oneness with Him. To quote his own words:

> That I want thee, only thee—let my heart repeat without

end. All desires that distract me, day and night, are false and empty to the core.

As the night keeps hidden in its gloom the petition for light, even thus in the depth of my unconsciousness rings the cry—'I want thee, only thee'.[17]

Thus, Tagore shows a close affinity with Kabir in his concept of God as both transcendent and immanent, cosmic and non-cosmic. Both the poets demonstrate that God is, as a matter of fact, beyond the notion of *nirguna* and *saguna*. However, while Kabir has a definite predilection for the *nirguna* God, Tagore shows inclination towards the *saguna* nature of God. But both the mystic poets bother little about the proofs of God's existence, for they consider the felt experience of God's reality more significant than the traditional proofs of His existence. Again, both have the conviction that to attain union with God, the renunciation of the world is not at all necessary; rather, in their view, men can reach God by discarding desires, vices and lust. Both of them assert that it is possible to accomplish this by means of love, evolution and dedication.

Again, in his view of soul, Tagore was influenced by Kabir to a large extent. According to Kabir, the whole cosmos is permeated by the Supreme Soul, i.e. God, and he lays stress on the oneness of this Supreme Soul and human soul which is the main principle of monism. The human soul, an integral part of the Supreme Soul is separated from the latter by illusion (*maya*). He elaborates the idea by giving the analogy of the pitcher of clay floating in the river. The water inside the pitcher is separated, and seems different from the water outside it, though the water is the same, but the moment the pitcher breaks, the water inside it becomes one with the water outside it. likewise, the human soul is alienated from the Supreme Soul by illusion, but the moment this pitcher of illusion is shattered, the human soul becomes one with the Supreme Soul, the Brahma. The oneness thus achieved eliminates all kinds of distinctions between 'I' and 'Thou', the subject and the object, the lover the beloved, etc. This oneness givės man the supreme vision which fills him with blessedness. In the words of Kabir translated into English by Tagore:

> He Himself is the tree, the seed, and the germ
>
> He Himselve is the flower, the fruit, and the shade.
>
> He Himself is the sun, the light, and the lighted.
>
> He Himself is Brahma, creature, and Maya.
>
> He Himself is the manifold form, the infinite space;
>
> He is the breath, the word, and the meaning.
>
> He Himself is the limit and the limitless: and beyond both the limited and the limitless is He, the Pure Being.
>
> He is the Immanent Mind in Brahma and in the creature.
>
> The Supreme Soul is seen within the woul,
>
> The Point is seen within the Supreme Soul,
>
> And within the Point, the refection is seen again.
>
> Kabir is blest because he has this supreme vision![18]

Kabir repeatedly refers to the Supreme Soul residing within the human soul.

Kabir presents the human soul mainly as a woman passing through the various stages of life as a virgin, as a bride or beloved, as a separated woman pining for her lover or husband and as a chaste faithful woman. The love between the human soul and the Supreme Soul is eternal and constant. Kabir says:

> How could the love between Thee and me sever?
>
> From the beginning until the ending of time, there is love between Thee and me; and how shall such love be extinguished?
>
> Kabir says: 'As the river enters into the ocean, so my heart touches Thee.'[19]

In the state of union, the finite soul is bereft of all sense-experiences, thoughts and feelings, an is completely merged into the Supreme Soul, believing firmly that it hears, sees, feels, etc. only through the Eternal Soul. Kabir describes this mystical union of the finite and infinite souls in this manner:

> I have learned from Him how to walk without feet, to see without eyes, to hear without ears, to drink without mouth, to fly without wings;
>
> I have brought my love and my meditation into the land where there is no sun and moon, nor day and night.
>
> Without eating, I have tasted of the sweetness of nectar, and without water, I have quenched my thirst.[20]

Human soul as beloved separated from the Everlasting in the state of sleep of ignorance is painted in utter agony and restlessness by Kabir after the style of the mystics all over the world. To quote his own words:

> When I am parted from my Beloved, my heart is full of misery: I have no comfort in the day, I have no sleep in the night. To whom shall I tell my sorrow?
>
> The night is dark; the hours slip by. Because my Lord is absent, I start up and tremble with fear.
>
> Kabir says 'Listen, my friend! There is no other satisfaction, save in the encounter with the Beloved.'[21]

In the vein of Kabir, Tagore affirms that human soul is both united with, and separated from, the Eternal. The human soul, an integral part of the Supreme Soul, lives in separation as a result of the latter's intention: the Everlasting divides Himself into many shapes temporarily. Tagore, therefore, writes:

> Thou settest a barrier in thine own being and then earliest thy severed self in myriad notes. This thy self-separation has taken body in me.
>
> . . . .
>
> . . . .

> The great pageant of thee and me has overspread the sky. With the tune of thee and me all the air is vibrant, and all ages pass with the hiding and seeking of thee and me.[22]

Thus the separation between the Universal Soul and the individual soul is only an illusion, and this is how the eternal play between the infinite and the finite goes on. Inevitably, the ultimate end of human soul is to achieve oneness with the divine soul, and it is possible only by eradicating the narrow limitations of self, of ego. Man's selfish desires and worldly possessions are his fetters and limitations depriving the human of the union with the Infinite. The only obsessive need of the human soul is to achieve oneness with the Infinite Soul, but so long as it is enveloped by ego and worldly desires, it fails to attain the goal and lives in utter misery, restlessness and unhappiness. The human soul cannot have even the awareness of its immortality so long as it is a prisoner of selfishness, ego, desires possessions, etc.

Patently, Tagore is of the view that human soul can find supreme fulfilment and salvation only in the permanent company of the Infinite. This is why, he says in one of the songs of *Gitanjali*:

> Away from the sight of thy face my heart knows no rest nor respite, and my work becomes an endless toil in a shoreless sea of toil.[23]

The human soul can merge itself into the Infinite only by means of true and pure love which teaches the former to surrender itself completely to the latter. No wonder Tagore writes:

> From the blue sky an eye shall gaze upon me and summon me in silence. Nothing will be left for me, nothing whatever, and utter death shall I receive at thy feet.[24]

This perfect harmony between the two souls, achieved through love, inevitably results in supreme joy. This fills human soul with all-embracing consciousness which leads to the complete fusion of the finite and the Infinite. About this Kabir says:

> The inward and the outward are become as one sky, the infinite and the finite are united: I am drunken with the sight of this All!
>
> This light of Thine fulfils the universe: the lamp of love that burns on the salver of knowledge.[25]

This is the state in which the individual soul becomes inalienable from the Infinite Soul or god. And it is in this way that human soul achieves self-transcendence, eternal life or fullness of life by perceiving the Infinite within it. Till human soul attains this ultimate, final goal, it wanders restlessly under the complete sway of worldiness, but once this object is achieved, it has all peace and joy.

Fears and doubts do not touch it, as it shares the eternal life which cannot be defeated or disturbed even by death. Tagore expresses this idea, having Kabirian echo, in the following words:

> When in the morning I looked upon the light I felt in a moment that I was no stranger in this world, that the inscrutable without name and form had taken me in its arms in the form of my own mother.
>
> Even so, in death the same unknown will appear as ever known to me, And because I love this life, I know I shall love death as well.[26]

However, like Kabir and many other Indian philosophers, Rabindranath Tagore thinks that the individual soul is able to attain this ideal state gradually. As a matter of fact, he takes quite a long time to reach the goal, and in the process has to pass through many lives. The very first song of *Gitanjali* is a spontaneous expression of this thought:

> Thou hast made me endless, such is thy pleasure. This

> frail vessel thou emptiest again and again, and fillest it ever with fresh life.
>
> This little flute of a reed thou hast carried over hills and dales, and hast breathed through it melodies eternally new.
>
> At the immortal touch of thy hands my little heart loses its limits in joy and gives birth to utterance ineffable.
>
> Thy infinite gifts come to me only on these very small hands of mine. Ages pass, and still thou pourest and still there is room to fill.[27]

The human soul, indeed, has to travel a very long distance through varied climes and religious for a very long period, incarnating inhuman forms several times, in order to attain the Absolute and become one with Him. In another song of *Gitanjali*, Tagore puts this idea in the following words:

> The time that my journey takes is long and the way of it long.
>
> I came out on the chariot of the first gleam of light, and pursued my voyage through the wildernesses of worlds leaving my track on many a start and planet.
>
> It is the most distant course that comes nearest to thyself, and that training is the most intricate, which leads to the utter simplicity of tune.
>
> The traveller has to knock at every alien door to come to his own, and one has to wonder through all the outer worlds to reach the innermost shrine at the end.[28]

But in this onward movement towards the final union, the individual soul has to pass through several physical forms, and this renewal of the body in which the soul has to reside before it becomes one with the Universal soul is named death. Thus death is only a step towards a fuller and higher life. Apropos of this Tagore sings:

> In the night of weariness let me give myself up to sleep without struggle, resting my trust upon thee.
>
> . . . .
>
> . . . .

It is thou who drawest the veil of night upon the tired eyes of the day to renew its sight in a fresher gladness of awakening.[29]

Like a true mystic, Rabindranath believes that the individual, finite soul is also the object of love of the Universal Soul. In fact, there is an incessant craving in the heart of the Eternal Spirit for the finite soul that continually waits for the arrival of the former. To quote Tagore's own words:

> This is my delight, thus to wait and watch at the wayside where shadow chases light and the rain comes in the wake of the summer.
>
> . . . .
>
> . . . .
>
> From dawn till dusk I sit here before my door, and I know that of a sudden the happy moment will arrive when I shall see.[30]

And at last the infinite Spirit is bound to embrace, love, and become one with the finite soul, leading the latter to ecstasy, and eternity, though only transitorily. The poet speaks of this as follows:

> ...and entering my heart unbidden even as one of the common crowd, unknown to me, my king, thou didst press the signet of eternity upon many a fleeting moment of my life.[31]

The love between the Universal Soul and the individual soul is mutual, and the latter, as has been said earlier, impatiently and indefatigably waits for the fulfilment in love and for the absolute and final union. Thus, almost imitating Kabir, Tagore writes about this mystic experience in these words:

> I am only waiting for love to give myself up at last into his hands. That is why it is so late and why I have been guilty of such omissions.

. . . .

. . . .

> The market day is over and work is all done for the busy. Those who came to call me in vain have gone back in anger. I am only waiting for love to give myself up at last into his hands.[32]

True, the real union between the human soul and the Everlasting is possible only through love and joy; it is a kind of spiritual marriage of the two souls—the finite and the infinite. The individual soul as a bride feels the ecstatic joy of this union with the Eternal, and in that alone it experiences a transcendental bliss, overflowing it with complete rest and absolute fulfilment very much in the way in which the river feels it while merging into the ocean. Of this bride-bridegroom relationship and of the final union of the two souls, Tagore sings as exquisitely as Kabir does:

> All that I am, that I have, that I hope and all my love have ever flowed towards thee in depth of secrecy. One final glance from thine eyes and my life will be ever thine own.
>
> The flowers have been woven and the garland is ready for the bridegroom. After the wedding the bride shall leave her home and meet her lord alone in the solitude of night.[33]

Thus we see that Tagore is immensely influenced by Kabir in his concept of human soul adopting several forms for the sake of achieving the final goal of uniting with the Everlasting Soul eternally. It assumes the form of a devotee, a beloved, a bride, etc. But Tagore slightly differs from Kabir in that the former is more obsessed with yearning and waiting than with the sense of fulfilment which often characterises Kabir's approach to the problem; in fact, Tagore is more a poet of separation than of union, Patently, in all of his celebrated poetical works such as *Gitanjali, Urvashi, Purabi, Meghdut,* dance dramas, etc., separation and hope for the meeting (*mahamilan*) are the main burden. In a word, the individual soul's agony of separation, longing for union with the Eternal and the realisation of the Divine are the dominant notes of his writings.

True, Tagore was so much impressed by Kabir that in his poetical masterpieces one can easily trace this influence. The nature of life, the mystical joy, the sense of inadequacy as a mystic, a desire for death, the devout dedication to God, a dislike for material allurements, the befriending of the companionless people on the earth, the wailing of the poet's heart—all these find poetic and direct expression in his works. Rabindranath's *magnum opus, Gitanjali*, is poetry of detachment from the material world. It is an attempt to escape from the busy, earthly life of man. It is the supernatural regions, and not the earthly substances that allure and delight the poet's soul. Naturally, he signs:

> I know that the day will come when my sight of this earth shall be lost, and life will take its leave in silence, drawing the last curtain over my eyes.[34]

Like Kabir, Tagore also makes use of lotus very metaphorically and symbolically. Like him again, Tagore has addressed God as friend, lover, teacher, bridegroom and musician. In the following exquisite lyric of *Gitanjali* the echo of Kabir can be clearly marked:

> I know not how thou singest, my master!
>
> I ever listen in silent amazement.
>
> The light of thy music illumines the world. The life breath of thy music runs from sky to sky. The holy stream of thy music breaks through all stony obstacles and rushes on.
>
> My heart longs to join in thy song, but vainly struggles for a voice. I would speak, but speech breaks not into song, and I cry out baffled. Ah, thou hast made my heart captive in the endless meshes of thy music, my master:[35]

Tagore asserts that God is the master musician. Sweet

music results from the harmony of notes and such a harmony is brought about by a skilled musician. This creation is the music of God, for it is the result of harmony and order imposed upon chaos which was nothing but a welter of discordant and warring elements. God is the master musician and this universe is this music. The poet listens to the music of his Master with amazement. His music illuminates the universe. He enlivens it from the sky to the earth by the life-breath of his song. Like a holy stream, His music rushes on overcoming all obstacles in the way. Even the stones are driven by the divine music. This divine music is compared to

(a) Light;

(b) Life Breath; and

(c) A strong current of water.

The poet yearns to meet God and sing with him. But he cannot do so. His voice fails him, and he cannot speak and sing. He cries out in extreme dismay and bewilderment. Human insignificance and imperfection as compared to the Divine is then brought out. The poet will like to become one with God, but he cannot do so because he is entrapped in this world or Maya which is the endless music of God. The sweet harmony of God's music is constantly sounded through the universe and the poet is held captive by it. He listens to it with rapturous joy and cannot free himself from its meshes. Kabir, as Tagore translated, says:

> Held by the cords of love, the swing of the Ocean of Joy sways to and fro; and a mighty sound breaks forth in song.
>
> . . . .
>
> . . . .
>
> Music is all around it, and there the heart partakes of the joy of the Infinite Sea.

Kabir says: "Dive thou into that Ocean of sweetness: thus let all errors of life and of death flee away.'[36]

Both Kabir and Tagore have addressed God as master musician for whose company the individual soul pines. Tagore' following lyric also expresses the intense yearning of the human soul for the reunion with the Divine:

> In the deep shadows of the rainy July, with secret steps thou walkest, silent as night, eluding all watchers.
>
> Today the morning has closed its eyes, heedless of the insistent calls of the loud east wind, and a thick veil has been drawn over the ever-wakeful blue sky.
>
> The woodlands have hushed their songs, and doors are all shut at every house. Thou art the solitary wayfarer in this deserted street. Oh my only friend, my best beloved, the gates are open in my house—do not pass by like a dream.[37]

The poet assumes the role of the beloved and God is the Lover Lord and Master, who is inseparable from him and the entire universe, and yet is strange and unknowable. Naturally, Kabir affirms:

> O How may I ever express that secret word?
>
> O how can I say He is not like this, and He is like that?
>
> If I say that He is within me, the universe is ashamed:
>
> If I say that He is without me, it is falsehood.
>
> He makes the inner and the outer worlds to be indivisibly one;
>
> The conscious and the unconscious, both are His footstools.
>
> He is neighter manifest nor hidden, He is neighter revealed nor unrevealed.
>
> There are not words to tell that which He is.[38]

In the following lovely song, Tagore, like Kabir, has

also used several words and images symbolically to convey ideas reverberating with the echoes of Kabir:

> I Thought I should ask of thee - but I dared not—the rose wreath thou hadst on thy neck. Thus I waited for the morning, when thou didst depart, to find a few fragments on the bed. And like a beggar I searched in the dawn only for a stray petal or two.
>
> Ah me, what is it I find? What token left of thy love? It is no flower, no spices, no vase of perfumed water. It is thy mighty sword, flashing as a flame, heavy as a bolt of thunder. The young light of morning comes through the window and spreads itself upon thy bed. The morning bird twitters and asks, "Woman, what hast thou got?' No, it is no flower, no spices, nor vase of perfumed water—it is thy dreadful sword.
>
> I sit and muse in wonder, what gift is this of thine. I can find no place where to hide it. I am ashamed to wear it, frail as I am, and it hurts me when I press it to my bosom, Yet shall I bear in my heart this honour of the burden of pain this gift of thine.
>
> From now there shall be no fear left for me in this world, and thou shall be victorious in all my strife. Thou hast left death for my companion and I shall crown him with my life. Thy sword is with me to cut asunder my bonds, and there shall be no fear left for me in the world.
>
> From now I leave off all petty decorations. Lord of my heart, no more shall there be for me waiting and weeping in corners, no more coyness and sweetness of demeanour. Thou hast given me thy sword for adornment. No more doll's decorations for me![39]

The poem of Kabir, translated beautifully by Tagore and cited below, males a very suggestive and meaningful use of the words 'sword', 'fight', 'battlefield', etc. which have unfailingly caught the attention of Rabindranath:

> Lay hold on your sword, and join in the fight.
> Fight, O my brother, as long as life lasts.

> Strike off your enemy's head, and there make an end of him quickly: then come, and bow your head at your King's Durbar.
>
> He who is brave, never forsakes the battle: he who flies from it is no true fighter.
>
> In the field of this body a great war goes forward, against passion, anger, pride, and greed:
>
> It is in the kingdom of truth, contentment and purity, that this battle is raging; and the sword that rings forth most loudly is the sword of His Name.[40]

To Tagore and Kabir, the sword is a Divine present and is given to man to fight all vices, such as pride and greed. True, the sword is used symbolically by both Tagore and Kabir.

Again, in the following song, Tagore has taken from Kabir the imagery of the musk deer:

> On the day when the lotus bloomed, alas, my mind was straying, and I knew it not. My basket was empty and the flower remained unheeded.
>
> Only now and again a sadness fell upon me, and I started up from my dream and felt a sweet trace of a strange fragrance in the south wind.
>
> That vague sweetness made my heart ache with longing and it seemed to me that it was the eager breath of the summer seeking for its completion.
>
> I know not than that it was so near, that it was mine, and that this perfect sweetness had blossomed in the depth of my own heart.[41]

Employing the image of musk and deep Kabir has said: "The musk is in the deer, but it seeks it not within itself: it wanders in quest of grass."[42] According to both Kabir and Tagore, God is inside man and man, like the musk deer, searches Him there where He is not. The influence of Kabir can thus, be seen repeatedly on the poetry of Rabindranath Tagore.

The entire discussion of Kabir's impact on Tagore in this chapter is based not on mere conjecture but on facts. There is evidence that the latter was the first to assign the former his rightful place in literature and society by revealing to the world the real nature and significance of his writings. Before Tagore nobody seriously thought of bringing out an authentic version of Kabir's poetry. At the beginning of the present century he made Acharya Kahitmohan Sen of *Visva-Bharati* prepare an authentic collection of Kabir's major poetical works, and it was only after this that the two renowned Hindi scholars, Dr. Shyam Sunder Das and Dr. Ram Kumar Verma, separately published Kabir's poetical works in Hindi, Not only did Tagore encourage Acharya Sen to bring out the first authentic collection of Kabir's poems, but he himself translated one hundred poems of Kabir into English so as to spread the significance of Kabir's thoughtful poetry throughout India and the world, thus showing his deep indebtedness to the great saint-poet of the fifteenth century. What is remarkable about Tagore's selection of these one hundred poems is that these are either about Kabir's scathing attack on idol-worship, religious rituals and caste feelings or about his ideal of religious synthesis, universal love and spiritual oneness. No wonder his slender book, *One Hundred Poems of Kabir,* was warmly received and eulogized all over the world. About this the following comments appeared in *Hartford Post*:

> The trend of Mr. Tagore's mystical genious makes him a peculiarly sympathetic interpreter of Kabir's vision and thought, and the book is perhaps one of the most important which that famous Hindu has introduced to the Western World.[43]

Tagore further evidenced his indebtedness to Kabir by asking Acharya Hazari Prasad Dwivedi to evaluate Kabir correctly and dispassionately so as to give a deadly blow to the erroneous judgement of Hndi critics on Kabir, particularly that of Acharya Ram Chandra Shukla who had estimated Kabir very faultily and casually by calling him *fakkar,* a carefree man, who had composed poetry, studded with metaphore and allegorical utterances, having nothing new but only word-jugglery meant to attract unducated people.[44] Written at Santiniketan under the inspiration of Tagore, Acharya Hazari Prasad Dwivedi's book on Kabir is indubitably the best critical work on the subject till to-day, and is fully successful in demolishing all the prejudices and erroneous remarks against the great saint poet. This celebrated Hindi scholar rightly observes about Kabir:

> He firmly believes that the dazzling brightness of the Kabir's poems cannot be subjected to intellectual dissection. It is not something which can be preserved in a museum, but is a living thing. Many books have been written on Kabir and many more will be written but only a few may get at the depth of his profundity.[45]

NOTES AND REFERENCES

1. Ernest Rhys, *Rabindranath Tagore,* p. 18.
2. Rabindranath Tagore, *One Hundred Poems of Kabir* (Madras; Macmillan Pocket Tagore Edition, 1988), pp.63-4.
3. *Ibid.,* pp. 64-5.
4. *Ibid.,* pp. 21-2
5. Rabindranath Tagore, *One Hundred Peomes of Kabir,* pp. 24-5.
6. Rabindranath Tagore, *Gitanjali,* pp 18-9.
7. Rabindranath Tagore, *The Religion of Man,* p. 58.
8. *Gitanjali,* pp. 38-9.
9. *Ibid.,* pp. 6-7.
10. *One Hundred Poems of Kabir,* p. 26.
11. *Ibid.,* pp. 49-50.
12. *Ibid.,* pp. 24-5.

13. *Gitanjali,* pp. 63-4.
14. S. Radhakrishnan, *The Philosophy of Rabindranath Tagore* (Baroda: Good Companions, 1958), p. 42.
15. *Gitanjali,* p. 42.
16. *Ibid.,* p. 8.
17. *Ibid.,* p. 22.
18. *One Hundred Poems of Kabir,* pp. 24-5.
19. *Ibid.,* p. 45.
20. *Ibid.,* p. 41.
21. *Ibid.,* 55-6.
22. *Gitanjali,* pp. 47-8.
23. *Ibid.,* p. 4.
24. *Ibid.,* p. 65.
25. *One Hundred Poems of Kabir,* p. 35.
26. *Gitanjali,* p. 63.
27. *Ibid.,* pp.1-2.
28. *Ibid.,* pp. 7-8.
29. *Ibid.,* p. 15.
30. *Ibid.,* p. 26.
31. *Ibid.,* pp. 25-6.
32. *Ibid.,* pp. 10-1.
33. *Ibid.,* pp. 60-1.
34. *Ibid.,* p. 61.
35. *Ibid.,* pp. 2-3.
36. *One Hundred Poems of Kabir,* pp. 31-2.
37. *Gitanjali,* p. 13.

38. *One Hundred Poems of Kabir*. P. 26.

39. *Gitanjali*, pp. 33-4.

40. *One Hundred Poems of Kabir*, p. 47.

41. *Gitanjali*, p. 12.

42. *One Hundred Poems of Kabir*, p. 24.

43. Cited by Ernst Rhys in *Rabindranath Tagore*, p. 18.

44. Acharya Ram Chandra Shukla, *History of Hindi Literature* (Kashi; Nagari Pracharni Sabha, 1962), p. 81.

45. Acharya Hazardi Prasad Dwivedi, *Kabir* (Delhi: Rajkamal Prakashan, 1971), p. 227.

4

Other Indian Influences on Tagore: Vaishnava Poets

A sensitive artist is inevitably influenced by his surroundings. Rabindranath, endowed with a very impressionable creative mind, was not an exception to it. As such, his familiarity with the Vaishnava poets early in his life left a lasting impact on his mind and hence a deep mark on his writings. Obviously time and again, we perceive the echoes of eminent Vaishnava poets, particularly Jayadeva, Vidyapati and Chandidas, on his poetry. He came in touch with the old Vaishnava poetry of the medieval times through Babu Akshay Sarkar and Saroda Mitter who collected and published a series of old Vaishnava poetry. Rabindranath was fascinated by this poetry though he had to confront with the problem of comprehending fully the meaning of this poetry because it was largely in the Maithili language which was not his mother tongue. Commenting on his innate love for the old Vaishnava poets, Rabindranath writes in *Reminiscences*:

> My feeling towards them was that same eager curiosity with which I regarded the unger-minated sprout within the seed, or the undiscovered mystery under the dust-covering of the earth. My enthusiasm was kept up with the hope of bringing to light some unknown poetical gems, as I went deeper and deeper into the unexplored darkness of this treasure house.[1]

It was Rabindranath's father from whom he inherited a profound interest in the Vaishnava poets, particularly

Jayadeva. While only a child he accompanied his father on a trip on the Ganges in his houseboat, and it was during this short outing that he saw an old Fort William edition of Jayadeva's master-piece, *Gitagovinda*, among his father's collection of books. Recalling the charm of his first looking into this piece of exquisite poetry on him, he confessed later on while at the height of his poetic powers and popularity:

> It was in the Bengali character. The verses were not printed in separate lines, but ran on like prose. I did not then know anything of Sanskrit, yet because of my knowledge of Bengali many of the words were familiar. I cannot tell how often I read that *Gita Govinda*. I can well remember this line:
>
> The night that was passed in the lonely forest cottage.
>
> It spread an atmosphere of vague beauty over my mind. That one Sanskrit word Nibhritanikunja-griham, meaning 'the lonely forest cottage,' was quite enough for me.
>
> I had to discover for myself the intricate metre of Jayadeva, because its divisions were lost in the clumsy prose form of the book. And this discovery gave me very great delight. Of course I did not fully comprehend Jayadeva's meaning. It would hardly be correct to aver that I had got it even partly. But the sound of the words and the lilt of the metre filled my mind with pictures of wonderful beauty, which impelled me to copy out the whole of the book for my own use.[2]

Consequently, as teenager Rabindranath's imagination was so much caught by the Vaishnava poets that his initial attempts at writing poetry were simply an imitation of these medieval poets. He remembers one of his earliest poems written in imitation of these poets. It was composed in maithili beginning like this "*Gahana kusuma kunja majhe...*" He was so much overjoyed by it that he read it out to the first person he met and was immensely delighted by the praise he accorded to it. This infused him with the impetus to write more and more poems of this kind under the influence of the Vaishnava poets. Under the pseudonym of Bhanu Singha, he collected these poems and showed them to his friend well-versed in Maithili. The poems moved him so much so that he rapturously exclaimed: "'These could not have been written even by *Vidyapati* or *Chandidas*!' ... ' I really must have that Ms. to make over to Akshay Babu for publication.'"[3] Later on, these poems appeared in the *Bharati*, and Dr. Nishikanta Chatterjee, the poet's friend, assigned these lyrics a significant place in his doctoral thesis on comparative study of Indian and European lyric poetry on which he was awarded the degree of Ph.D. in Germany. Even in his later life, when Rabindranath was able to find and express his own poetic idiom and was, more or less, above direct influences of this kind, he could not ignore the value of the veracity and genuineness of emotions embodied in the old Vaishnava poetry. Apropos of this, he states at one place in *Reminiscences*:

> The language might have passed muster; for that which the old poets wrote in was not their mother tongue, but an artificial language varying in the hands of different poets. But there was nothing artificial about their sentiments.[4]

When Rabindranath Tagore, returned home from his second voyage to England and spent some very happy days amidst very lovely natural surroundings at a river-side villa at Chandernagore in the company of his brother and sister-in-law, he was often haunted by the exquisite Vaishnava songs which he would recite to his immense delight in accompaniment to harmonium. He records it as follows: "Some rainy afternoons I spent in a veritable frenzy, singing away old *Vaishnava* songs to my own tunes, accompanying myself on a harmonium."[5] He not only composed a good deal of his early poetry in imitation of the old Vaishnava poetry and often sang it with ecstasy, but also wrote one of his earliest critical pieces in spontaneous, effusive appreciation of the Vaishnava lyrics of the medieval age in the well-known monthly magazine, *prachar* (the Preacher) of which Bankim Babu was the editor.[6]

The above discussion bears a testimony to the fact that Rabindranath's poetic, critical and devotional faculties were greatly shaped by the medieval Vaishnava poetry. But, as has already been hinted, of all the old Vaishnava poets, he was most deeply indebted to three poets, Jayadeva, Vidyapati and Chandidas. Their formal excellence, metrical perfection, lyrical excellence and loveliness of images possessed the creative genius of Rabindranath so much that these clearly influenced even his mature writings including *Gitanjali*. The echoes and impact of these poets, particularly of Jayadeva the author of *gitagovinda*, are easily perceptible in the theme, emotion, characters, *sahaj bhakti* (natural devotion), philosophy, symbols, atmosphere, etc. of Rabindranath Tagore's *magnum opus, Gitanjali*. Thus a close perusal of the two poetical works—*Gitagovida* and *Gitanjali*—in juxtaposition with each other is essential to prove the validity of this assertion.

Thematically, Rabindranath Tagore's poetry, especially *Gitanjali*, evinces the impact and echoes of the Vaishnava poetry. Tagore's acme of poetic achievement has the thematic pattern of union-separation-reunion which seems to be an imitation of the great Vaishnava poetry. *Gitanjali* opens with the recollections of the earlier union and concludes with the prospective union, and in - between the two there is bitterness of separation flanked by the unforgettable memories of the past union and the sweet expectations of the rapturous reunion. As a matter of fact, this is the core of Indian philosophy. Thus in the Vedanta the cosmic self is the ultimate reality, the world is illusion, and '*maya*' is the separation of human soul from the Eternal. Again, according to the *Sankhya* philosophy, the human is *Jiva*, the ultimate is *Furusa* and *Prakriti* is the alienating force and process of the two, the reunion of whom is the final end of human life. Likewise, the old Vaishnava poetry is centred upon the relationship of Radha and Krishna, standing for *Jiva* and *Purusa* respectively, and also spotlighting the process of union, separation and reunion, and the emancipation from it forever through complete attachment with the Eternal. Thus Jayadeva's Radha has the reminiscences of the earlier love relationships with Krishna:

> Meeting me under a flowering tree, he calms my fear of dark time,
> Delighting me deeply by quickly glancing looks at my heart:
>
> My heart recalls Hari here in his love dance,
> Playing seductively, laughing, mocking me.[7]

In the same vein, Tagore, presenting himself as the devotee-lover, recollects his past union with the Infinite and records its joyous effect on him in the very first song of *Gitanajali*, thus:

> At the immortal touch of thy hands my little heart loses its limits in joy and gives birth to utterance ineffable.[8]

It is, therefore, impossible for him to forget the thrill and sensations overflowing his entire being as a result of his physical and spiritual contacts with the Divine. Apropos of this, he says:

> I have tasted of the hidden honey of this lotus that expands on the ocean of light, and thus am I blessed—
>
> . . . .
>
> . . . .
>
> My whole body and my limbs have thrilled with his touch who is beyond touch; and if the end comes here, let it come—let this be my parting word.[9]

Obliterating himself completely in the company of the Eternal, he only felt fathomless joy without bothering to know anything about his intimate partner in love-making:

> When my play was with thee I never questioned who thou wert. I knew nor shyness nor fear, my life was boisterous.
>
> In the early morning thou wouldst call me from my sleep like my own comrade and lead me running from glade to glade.
>
> On those days I never cared to know the meaning of songs thou sangest to me. Only my voice took up the tunes, and my heart danced in their cadence.[10]

The devotee-lover's carefree, rapturous life without coyness and fear are reminiscient of the Vaishnava poets' depiction of Radha's and Gopies' running after Krishna and experiencing the innermost depths of the ecstasy of love-making. Jayadeva's *Gitagovinda* ends with Radha's profound, tranquil joy of passionate love-making with Krishna and with her deep desire for getting every part of her body touched and decorated with ornaments by the Lord Himself. Likewise, *Gitanjali* concludes with the poet-lover's unflinching belief in the final, everlasting meeting with the Divine:

> In one salutation to thee, my God, let all my senses spread out and touch this world at thy feet.
>
> Like a rain-cloud of July hung low with its burden of unshed showers let all my mind bend down at thy door in one salutation to thee.
>
> . . . .
>
> . . . .
>
> Like a flock of homesick cranes flying night and day back to their mountain nests let all my life take its voyage to its eternal home in one salutation to thee.[11]

The lover's craving for the final union with the infinite has the touch of the erotic ecstasy experienced by Radha in the desire to meet and love Krishna eternally. Obviously,

Rabindranath is influenced by the Vaishnava poets so far as the central idea of most of his poetry is concerned.

The Vaishnava philosophy is clearly reflected in Tagore's poetry. The Vaishnavism of *Sahajivas* is imbedded in the monism of the *Upanishads,* according to which, all is one, but this one, i.e. *Brahma,* divides itself into two: Krishna, the *Bhagvat,* and Radha, his *Shakti*. Krishna and Radha are one and the same, though, for the sake of heavenly sport, they incarnate themselves in two distinct physical entities. The foundation of this Vaishnava philosophy is the belief in manifold infinite powers of Lord-Krishna, usually put in three categories named as : *Jiva-Shakti, Maya-Shakti* and *Chit-Shakti*.

Jiva-Shakti is the power which enables human soul to come in contact with the everlasting. Krishna the *Bhagvat* is the embodiment of fire, while the individual souls (*jives*) are like eternal sparks of the everlasting fire. The relationship between the two is called, in philosophical terminology, *bhedabheda* which means that the two, though the same, have distinct entities. Naturally, this monism is dualistic and hence a mystery and is beyond analysis (*achintya*). Influenced by the Vaishnava philosophy, Rabindranath sings of this relationship between the *Jiva* and the *Bhagvat* in the following manner:

> Thou set test a barrier in thine own being and then callest thy severed self in myriad notes. This thy self-separation has taken body in me.
>
> The great pageant of thee and me has overspread the sky. With the tune of thee and me all the air is vibrant, and all ages pass with the hiding and seeking of thee and me.[12]

According to Vaishnavism, the empirical world comes into being as a result of the power of illusion, *maya*. This *maya,* which governs the *Jiva,* is controlled by the *Bhagvat,* and the people of the world are able to get rid of the shackles of it only by means of devotion to the *Bhagvat*. Speaking of this, Jayadeva writes poetically thus;

> Watching with long omniscient lotus-petal eyes, You free us from bonds of existence, Preserving life in the world's three realms, Triumph, God of Triumph, Hari:[13]

Rabindranath Tagore expresses his belief in this *maya-shakti*, the power of illusion of the *Bhagvat* in these lines of *Gitanjali*;

> That I should make much of myself and turn it on all sides, thus casting coloured shadows on thy radiance— such is thy *maya*.[14]

In the same vein, he again sings of it in another lyric more emphatically:

> He it is who weaves the web of this *maya* in evanescent hues of gold and silver, blue and green, and lets peep out through the folds his feet, at whose touch I forget myself.[15]

The *Chit* or *swarupa-shakti*, the highest form of which is labelled the *haladini-shakti*, the power of joy, means the limitless power of the *Bhagvat* to give and enjoy delight. Thus the Vaishnavas believe that Krishna is the every incarnation of joy, and Radha is the *haladini-shakti* of Krishna by means of which he gives and tastes delight. No wonder Krishna, as painted by Jayadeva in *Gitagovida*, "delights everybody", "bestowing bliss every where". Pinning his faith in this aspect of Vaishnavism, Rabindranath presents God as the very embodiment of bliss:

> Light, my light, the world-filling light, the eye-kissing light heart-sweetening light!
>
> Ah, the light dances, my darling, at the centre of my life; the light strikes, my darling, the chords of my love; the sky opens, the wind runs wild, laughter passes over the earth.
>
> . . . .
>
> . . . .
>
> Mirth spreads from leaf to leaf, my darling, and gladness without measure. The heaven's river has drowned its

> banks and the flood of joy is abroad.[16]

In several of the Vaishnava works, specially in Gitagoinda, Krishna is repeatedly portrayed delighting Radha with his love-play and being thrilled by her. Rabindranath Tagore, too, paints God engaged in similar kind of act with the human soul:

> What divine drink wouldst thou have, my God, from this overflowing cup of my life?
>
> . . . .
>
> . . . .
>
> Thy world is weaving words in my mind and thy joy is adding music to them. Thou givest thyself to me in love and then feelest thine own entire sweetness in me.[17]

According to the Vaishnava philosophy, the attainment of the final emancipation is possible only through attachment. Thus this philosophical system believes that attachment is not a hindrance in the way of emancipation, but is the means to achieve it. This is the reason why the *Bhagvat* is presented as a lover and it is only by having love and attachment for him that the devotee can reach near and attain, the Infinite. It is by loving and desiring Krishna without thinking of liberation that man can get liberation. Apparently, liberation, in the view of the Vaishnava thinkers, is not the end of love, but only its by-product. The 'secret love' of *sahajivas* stands for the emancipation from the world through attachment to the world. Since love is higher than liberation, the Vaishnava philosophy has no belief in actual, final union because if it is attained and the devotee is liberated, there shall be no devotion and no love. This faith is poetically expressed by Jayadeva in these words:

> Krishna, demon Kamsa's foe,
> Feeling Radha bind his heart with chains
> Of memories buried in other worldly lives,
> Abandoned the beautiful cowherd girls.[18]

Likewise, Rabindranath Tagore rejects that liberation which alienates the devotes from the Everlasting, for even the *Bhagvat* is attached to this world, this creation. To quote Tagore's own words:

> Deliverance? Where is this deliverance to be found? Our master himself has joyfully taken upon him the bonds of creation; he is bound with us all for ever.[19]

Infact, while love is bondage and attachment, all religious and philosophical systems are usually preoccupied with liberation. However, the Vaishnava poets hold that Krishna is the lord of the cosmos, but He becomes a part of time and space owing to his love for Radha, thus binding Himself to the temporal and spatial world. Patently, these medieval poets regarded play or *leela* as the 'creative' and 'recreative' activity of the Lord, and worship as a blissful aspect of the divine *leela*. The object of God's play is nothing else but the play itself. The world is His playground, and His play consists of generation, operation, destruction and then regeneration. This *leela* becomes the primary object of the singing and meditation of His devotees. In the opinion of the Vaishnava poets, women called *Gopies* are most fit for joining this leela, though men, of course, are not unfit for it. His devotees are His friends during the day time, but they become His beloveds during the night. Men don't commit any sin by joining His play, for He is neither male nor female but is transcendent. However, the play takes place in the consciousness of the meditator. Naturally, the emotion of the play is a mental experience, and not merely the physical one. No wonder Jayadeva writes in *Gitagovinda*:

> When he quickens all things
> To create bliss in the world,
> His soft black sinuous lotus limbs
> Begin the festival of love
> And beautiful cowdherd girls wildly
> Wind him in their bodies.

Friend, in spring young Hari plays
Like erotic mood incarnate.[20]

Under the impact of the Vaishnava poets, Rabindranath paints the world as the playground of the world in these words:

> In this playhouse of infinite forms I have had my play and here have I caught sight of him that is formless.[21]

Again, in another song, Rabindranath Tagore expresses the same idea identical to that of the Vaishnava poets:

> Thus it is that thy joy in me is so full. Thus it is that thou hast come down to me. O thou lord of all heavens, where would be thy love if I were not?
>
> Thou hast taken me as thy partner of all this wealth. In my heart is the endless play of thy delight. In my life thy will is ever taking shape.[22]

The influence of the Vaishnava poets on Ravindranath Tagore is traceable in asmuch as he presents his God very much like the Krishna of the earlier poets, though never calling the Eternal by that name, He depicts God playing upon the flute like Lord Krishna as is evident in the very first song of *Gitanjali*:

> This little flute of a reed thou hast carried over hills and dales, and hast breathed through it melodies eternally new.[23]

Then, in the third song of this poetic work of global fame, Rabindranath paints God as eternal singer enthralling and captivating all human souls by His divine music very much like Lord Krishna intoxicating all by his musical flute-playing. In the words of the poet:

> I know not how thou singest, my master! I ever listen in silent amazement.
>
> The light of thy music illumines the world. The life breath of thy music runs from sky to sky. The holy stream of thy music breaks through all stony obstacles and rushes on.

> My heart longs to join in thy song, but vainly struggles for a voice. I would speak, but speech breaks not into song, and I cry out baffled. Ah, thou hast made my heart captive in the endless meshes of thy music, my master![24]

In the seventh song of *Gitanjali*, the poet wishes to be "like a flute of reed for thee to fill with music."[25] Again, lyrics XXI, XXVI, XXVII, LXXIV and LXXIX depict God in the garb of Lord Krishna ceaselessly immersed in music. The Vaishnava poetry repeatedly paints Lord Vishnu as a playful cowherd-lower, thus humanizing the Supreme Being. Following this concept of the Divine, Rabindranath Tagore portrays God as the humanized Krishna of *Gitagovinda*, and not as the Absolute, Impersonal *Brahman* of the *Upanishads*. In the Vaishnava poetry, both Radha and Krishna long for the love of each other and feel the pangs of separation in love. No wonder like Radha, Krishna also suffers the pain of separation and pines for the beloved:

> Sighing incessantly, he pours out his grief. He endlessly searches the empty directions. Each time he enters the forest thicket, Humming to himself, he gasps for breath. He makes your bed of love again and again, staring at it in empty confusion. Lovely Radha, your lover suffers Passion's mental pain.[26]

In the similar fashion, Tagore's God craves for the intimacy with the human soul. The poet, thus, writes:

> If I call not thee in my prayers, if I keep not thee in my heart, thy love for me still waits for my love.[27]

Again, Rabindranath gives vent to this belief in another lyric in these words:

> Thus it is that thou hast come down to me.
>
> O thou lord of all heavens, where would be thy love if I were not?[28]

Obviously, there is close resemblance between the Vaishnava poets' Krishna and Tagore's God, and this demonstrates the influence of the former on the latter. The Radha of the earlier poets can be seen in the devotee-lover of *Gitanjali*. Rabindranath evinces his feminine passionate love for God. Like Jayadeva's Radha who meets her lover Krishna in darkness secretly, the devotee-lover in *Gitanjali* sets out for the adventurous love-making in the darkness of the night in the cloudy rainy season. He seems to get the message for it from Lord lover. About this, the poet writes:

> Misery knocks at thy door, and her message is that thy lord is wakeful, and he calls thee to the love-tryst through the darkness of night.
>
> The sky is overcast with clouds and the rain is ceaseless. I know not what this is that stirs in me—I know not its meaning.
>
> A moment's flash of lighting drags down a deeper gloom on my sight, and my heart gropes for the path to where the music of the night calls me.[29]

Vidyapati's Radha seems to be the model of Tagore's devotee beloved as painted in the above lines, for the former, on getting a message from Sakhi, goes to meet Krishna secretly in torrential rains in the darkness of night in the month of July.

Like most of the Vaishnava poetry, the central emotion (Bhava) of Tagore's poetry is devotion (Bhakti) not as simple literal devotion, but as passionate, profound love. This kind of devotion (*Bhakti*), an integral part of the later Krishna cults, is not simple worship or meditation on God, but anurakti, i.e. fathomless affection or attachment, which, different from knowledge (*Gyan*) or action (*Karma*), is a feeling usually aiming at liberation. The later Vaishnava poets like Jayadeva deviated from this notion of devotion as love in that they considered human love as an ultimate reality in itself, rejecting the earlier idea of its being only a means of attaining liberation. In their opinion, each and every molecule of the body, heart and soul experiences and celebrates this love. Rabindranath Tagore imbibed this spirit of love, and eloquently expressed it in his poetry.

In fact, the emotion (*Bhava*) of love that pervades Tagore's poetry has an unmistakable kinship with that of the Vaishnava poetry. Tagore, like them, is preoccupied with the dynamics of union and separation in love. Following the Vaishnava poets, particularly Jayadeva, he paints an exquisite picture of the devotes-beloved's meeting with the Eternal- lover:

> What was the power that made me open out into this vast mystery like a bud in the forest at midnight:
>
> When in the morning I looked upon the light I felt in a moment that I was no stranger in this world, that the inscrutable without name and form had taken me in its arms...[30]

Rabindranath paints a rapturous picture of love-making, showing the beloved surrendering herself completely to the lover after the fashion of the Vaishnava poets. The two are in obsolute physical and emotional union, and so the beloved has removed her ornaments, and is in her purely naked self in order to become one with her lover. To quote the poet's own words.

> My song has put off her adornments. She has no pride of dress and decoration. Ornaments would mar our union; they would come between thee and me; their jingling would drown thy whispers.[31]

Time and again, we come across love-scenes such as these in the Vaishnava poetry. For instance, Jayadeva portrays Radha getting ready to put off her ornaments and dress in order to immerse fully in love-play with Krishna:

> Leave your noisy anklets: They clang like traitors in love play.

Go to the darkened thicket, friend : Hide in a cloak of night!

In woods on the wind-swept Jumna bank, Krishna waits in wildflower garlands.

. . . .

. . . .

Loosen your clothes, unite your belt, open your loins!

Radha, your gift of delight is like treasure in a bed of vines.

In woods on the wind-swept Jumna bank,

Krishna waits in wildflower garlands.[32]

The Vaishnava poetry is saturated with love-in-separation motif. Following this tradition, Tagore again and again dwells upon the pangs of separation in love. About these pangs of love in separation Tagore sings eloquently and enchantingly thus in *Gitanjali*:

> It is the pang of separation that spreads throughout the world and gives birth to shapes innumerable in the infinite sky.
>
> It is this sorrow of separation that gazes in silence all night from star to star and becomes lyric among rustling leaves in rainy darkness of July.
>
> It is this overspreading pain that deepens into loves and desires, into sufferings and joys in human homes; and this it is that ever melts and flows in songs through my poet's heart.[33]

In *Gitanjali,* we come across four of the seven stages of the beloved-in-grief-of-separation, *Virhani Naika*: *Prosita-Priya,* that is, the beloved whose lover is far away from her and it is difficult to reach near him; Vasak sajja, that is, the beloved who impatiently waits for her lover with intense longing and is keen to welcome him; *Vipralabdha,* that is, the lady love whose lover does not fulfil the promise of meeting her at a fixed time and place; and

Abhisarika, that is, the beloved who secretly goes to meet her lover in the darkness of night. The first type of the devotee-lover is described thus in *Gitanjali*:

> The time that my journey takes is long and the way of it long.
>
> I came out on the chariot of the first gleams of light, and pursued my voyage through the wilderenesses of worlds leaving my track on many a star and planet.
>
> It is the most distant course that comes nearest to thyself, and that training is the most intricate which leads to the utter simplicity of a tune.[34]

In *Gitanjali* the devotee as *Vasak Sajja* is painted waiting restlessly and expectantly for the Eternal Lover a number of times. For instance, in lyric XLIV, we come across the following exquisite picture of this kind of devotee-lover:

> From dawn till dusk I sit here before my door, and I know that of a sudden the happy moment will arrive when I shall see.[35]

Here it may be pointed out that Tagore owes a lot to Vidyapati. Songs IV and V in Canto 19 of *Vidyapati Padavali* show how Radha's heart is filled with delight as a result of the hope to meet Krishna, and she smiles, sings and conceives of numerous tricks for love-play.

The third stage of devotee-lover, labelled as Vipralabdha, is beautifully presented by Jayadeva in these words of aggrieved Radha:

> Just when we promised to meet, Hari avoided the woods.
>
> The flawless beauty of my youth is barren now. Whom can I seek for refuge here?
>
> My friend's advice deceives me.[36]

Equally admirable is Rabindranath's portrayal of this type of devotee-lover in *Gitanjali*:

> Early in the day it was whispered that we should sail in a boat, only thou and I, and never a soul in the world would know of this our pilgrimage to no country and to no end.
>
> . . . .
>
> . . . .
>
> Is the time not come yet? Are there works still to do? Do, the evening has come down upon the shore and in the fading light the seabirds come flying to their nests.[37]

Also, there is a lovely delineation of the devotee-lower called *Abhisarika* in Tagore's *Gitanjali,* very much after the style of the Vaishnava poets. In this context, the following extract can be cited:

> Light, oh where is the light ? Kindle it with the burning fire cf desire:
>
> There is the lamp but never a flicker of a flame—is such thy fate, my heart?
>
> Ah death were better by far for thee:
>
> . . . .
>
> . . . .
>
> The sky is overcast with clouds and the rain is ceaseless. I know not what this is that stirs in me—I know not its meaning.
>
> A moment's flash of lightning drags down a deeper gloom on my sight, and my heart gropes for the path to where the music of the night calls me.
>
> Light, oh where is the light! Kindle it with the burning fire of desire! It thunders and the wind rushes screaming through the void. The night is black as a black stone, Let not the hours pass by in the dark. Kindle the lamp of love with thy life.[38]

Here we notice the echoes of Vidyapati's description of *Abhisar* in song fourteen of Canto 12 of his *Padavali*. The older poet shows Radha going to meet Krishna in the dark night with lightning and torrential rains. She finds it very difficult to reach the place fixed for meeting Krishna.

The impact of the Vaishnava poetry on Tagore can also be clearly seen in the latter's portrayal of almost all the symptoms of love in separation as painted in Jayadeva's *Gitagovinda*—viz. longing (*Abhilasha*), fear (*Bhaya*), becoming one with the lover (*Tanmayata*), Remembrance (*Smarna*) and refuge (*Sharan*).

The first symptom of love in separation fraught with pain is again and again dealt with in *Gitanjali* much in the same manner in which Jayadeva does in *gitagovinda*. Abandoning her modesty, Jayadeva's Radha is completely preoccupied with the craving for the lover-meeting with Lord Krishna as is evident in the following extract:

> While you idle here, modesty abandons her,
> She laments, sobs as she waits to love you.
> Lord Hari,
> Radha suffers in her retreat.[39]

In the similar vein Rabindranath Tagore paints the devotee-beloved undergoing the fathomless pain of separation and living in the hope of meeting her lover. The lines, quoted below, bear witness to it:

> ... there is the agony of wishing in my heart.
>
> . . . .
>
> . . . .
>
> I live in the hope of meeting with him; but this meeting is not yet.[40]

Like the Radha of the Vaishnava poets, Tagore's devotee-beloved does not bother about the public condemnation, and openly waits for the Divine Lover. To quote his own words:

> I am only waiting for love to give myself up at last into his hands...

> They come with their laws and their codes to binn me fast; but I evade them ever, for I am only waiting for love to give myself up at last into his hands.
>
> People blame me and call me heedless; I doubt not they are right in their blame.[41]

Fears of all kinds, which the separated and alienated lovers inescapably experience, are repeatedly described poetically by the Vaishnava poets and Rabindranath Tagore. There is a very vivid, captivating picture of the devotee-beloved's heart surcharged with fear in the following lyric of *Gitanjali*:

> Clouds heap upon clouds and it darkens. Ah, love, why dost thou let me wait outside at the door all alone?
>
> In the busy moments of the noontide work I am with the crowd, but on this dark lonely day it is only for thee that I hope.
>
> If thou showest me not thy face, if thou leavest me wholly aside, I know not how I am to pass these long, rainy hours.
>
> I keep gazing on the far-away gloom of the sky, and my heart wanders wailing with the restless wind.[42]

The particular symptom of separation in love known as Tanmayata, i.e., the beloved's attempt to look like the lover and identify herself with him, is very frequently present in the Vaishnava poetry as well as in Tagore's poetical masterpieces. Thus, Jayadeva presents Radha dressed like Krishna and becoming one with him:

> Staring at her ornaments' natural grace,
> She fancies, "I am Krishna, Madhu's foe."
> Lord Hari,
> Radha suffers in her retreat.[43]

Moving a step further, Vidyapati paints Radha so deeply immersed in love with Krishna that she believes herself to be Krishna and repeatedly utters Radha's name passionately and pathetically. Rabindranath's poetry abounds in descriptions of this kind of intensity and frenzy of love depriving the lover of his individuality and entity completely. No wonder the devotee-beloved of *Gitanjali*, time and again, addresses the Divine Lover as his 'bride', 'beloved' and also 'male lover'.

Remembrance (*Smarna*) is the most patent feature of love in separation, for separation gives pain which is counterbalanced by the strange joy accompanying the remembrance of the sweet moments of the past union. Despite the pangs of separation and little hope of union in near future, the lover only remembers the partner and pines for his or her company alone. Tagore, thus, writes:

> That I want thee, only thee—let my heart repeat without end. All desires that distract me, day and night, are false and empty to the core.
>
> As the night keeps hidden in its gloom the petition for light, even thus in the depth of my unconsciousness rings the cry—'I want thee, only thee'.[44]

This brings to our mind Jayadeva's portrayal of Radha thinking obsessively of Krishna and feeling convinced of getting solace and comfort only in his company:

> She evokes you in deep meditation to reach your distant form.
>
> She laments, laughs, collapses, cries, trembles, utters her pain.
>
> Lying dejected by your desertion, fearing Love's arrows,
>
> She clings to you in fantasy, Madhava.[45]

The devotee-beloved impulsively seeks refuge in the Divine Lover as a result of deep dejection on account of separation from the latter. This submission to, and trust in, the Divine Lover is, as a matter of fact, the expression of love and devotion for the eternal Lover. The Vaishnava poets stress the value of separation for the realisation of the urge for refuge in, and union with, the Lord. Thus Jayadeva opens and closes his *magnum opus, Gitagovinda,* with the need for refuge in the Lord. The concluding lines run as follows:

> His musical skill, his meditation on Vishnu,
> His vision of reality in the erotic mood,
> His graceful play in these poems,
> All show that master-poet Jayadeva's soul
> Is in perfect tune with Krishna—
> Let blissful men of wisdom purify the world
> By singing his *gitagovinda.*
> Bhojadeva's heir, Ramdevi's son, Jayadeva,
> Expresses the power of poetry
> In the *Gitagovinda.*
> Let his poem be in the voice
> Of devotees like sage Parasara.[46]

Following the Vaishnava poets, Tagore does the same. Thus early almost at the beginning of *Gitanjali* the poet ejaculates:

> I touch by the edge of the far-spreading wing of my song thy feet which I could never aspire to reach.[47]

Then Tagore concludes his masterpiece with complete surrender to the Everlasting Lover, seeking refuge in His feet. To quote his own works:

> In one salutation to thee, my God, let all my senses spread out and touch this world at thy feet.
>
> Like a rain-cloud of July hung low with its burden of unshed showers let all my mind bend down at thy door in one salutation to thee
>
> . . . .
> . . . .
>
> Like a flock of homesick cranes flying night and day back to their mountain nests let all my life take its voyage to its eternal home in one salutation to thee.[48]

In the use of symbols Tagore evinces his indebtedness to the Vaishnava poets. Undoubtedly, has symbolic use of night, lotus and spring shows the influence of the medieval poets on him. According to the Indian literary conventions, darkness is erotic, for the night increases the erotic mood. No wonder then, if the Vaishnava poets and Tagore present darkness as contrast to light in order to symbolise the duality of flesh and spirit, *Jiva* and *atman*, male and female, etc. Apparently Jayadeva presents Radha ejaculating:

> I followed him at night to depths of the forest.
> He pierced my heart with arrows of love.
> Whom can I seek for refuge here?
> My friend's advice deceives me.[49]

This suggests that sexual desire is deadly, for it imprisons one within the shackles of this world, but this very negative thing may lead one to liberation in joy by the grace of the dark-complexioned Krishna. The darkness of ignorance is brightened by the devotion to Krishna just as the darkness of night is converted into joy by the beloved in the tryst. Tagore certainly appears to be possessed with the symbol of darkness as opposed to light, as is evident from the extract cited below:

> A moment's flesh of lightning drags down a deeper gloom on my sight, and my heart gropes for the path to where the music of the night calls me.
>
> Light, oh where is the light! Kindle it with the burning fire of desire ! It thunders and the wind rushes screaming through the void. The night is black as a black stone. Let not the hours pass by in the dark. Kindle the lamp of love with thy life.[50]

Thus, in Tagore's poetry, night, though standing for ignorance also, is unequivocally a symbol of increasing erotic mood. The lyrics numbering XXXVIII, XV, XVIII, XIX, XXIII, XXVI, XXVI, XXVIII, LI, and LXXVI are specially significant in regard to Tagore's symbolic use of night in his poetry.

The lotus is a very common symbol in Indian art and religion, and has been employed in varied ways. The Hindu religion presents it as a very sacred symbol, for the Lord Vishnu is believed to have it in one of his hands and it is also believed that it grows from his naval and on it resides Brahma who is the creator of the universe. The Vaishnava poets employ it metaphorically in more ways than one. For instance, we clearly see three modes of it in Jayadeva's *Gitagovinda*. In the first place, it is used as a sexual metaphor, as beauty and balm to give solace to the body tortured by powerful passion. The following lines can be quoted in support of it:

> While her body lies sick
> From smoldering fever of lover,
> Her heart suffers strange slow suffocation
> In mirages of sandalbalm, moonlight, *lotus pools*.[51]

Then the lotus is a psychological metaphor when it stands for consciousness as is clear from these lines:

> Weaving bracelets from supple lotus shoots
> As symbols of your skillful love, she keeps alive.
> Lord Hari
> Radha suffers in her retreat.[52]

Lastly, it represents the universe and is thus used as a cosmological metaphor. The following extract bears a testimony to it:

> See Hari on his cool couch of *moist lotuses*
> Reward your eyes with this fruit!
> Don't turn wounded pride on Madhava!
> He is proud too, sullen Radha.[53]

Rabindranath's poetry, too, is studded with the manifold symbolic uses of lotus. The following short quotation from *Gitanjali* evinces his wonderful symbolic genius imparting the lotus several layers of meaning:

> I surely know the hundred petals of a lotus will not remain closed for ever and the secret recess of its honey will be bared.[54].

In the above poetic piece, the poet refers to *Brahm-Randhra* through the lotus metaphor. The moment the head becomes the centre of consciousness, divine honey oozes out of it, and the human mind is transported to the state of ecstasy and cosmic consciousness. There may be another interpretation of the quotation; the erotic images are suggestive of sexual pleasure, for the female sexual organ is described as lotus in *Tantrism*.

In another lyric the image of lotus is employed in two senses: it stands for the sexual joy as well as the worldly life of this universe. Thus the lotus symbol becomes both the psychological as well as cosmological metaphor. The poetic lines run as follows:

> I have tasted of the hidden honey of this lotus that expands on the ocean of light, and thus am I blessed—[55]

Then in another song, "the open red lotus of pain"[56] is use as a cosmological metaphor by Rabindranath Tagore.

Both in the Vaishnava poetry as well as in Rabindranath Tagore's creative writings spring is usually symbolic of beauty, joy and repose. The lines, cited below from *Gitanjali*, fully support our assertion:

> The morning sea of silence broke into ripples of bird songs; and the flowers were all merry by the roadside; and the wealth of gold was scattered through the rift of the clouds while we busily went on our way and paid no heed.
>
> ....
>
> ....
>
> The sun rose to the mid sky and doves cooed in the shade. Withered leaves danced and whirled in the hot air

> of noon. The shepherd boy drowsed and dreamed in the shadow of the banyan tree, and I laid myself down by the water and stretched my tired limbs on the grass.
>
> ....
>
> ....
>
> The repose of the sun-embroidered green gloom slowly spread over my heart, I forgot for what I had travelled, and I surrendered my mind without struggle to the maze of shadows and songs.[57]

Obviously, this is the most suitable time for the lovers to meet and make love. Lyric LIV of *Gitanjali* presents a vivid picture of the lovers meeting in the spring season:

> I heard not thy steps as thou camest. Thine eyes were sad when they fell on me; thy voice was tired as thou spokest low—'Ah, I am a thirsty traveller' I started up from my day-dreams and poured water from my jar on thy joined palms. The leaves rustled overhead; the cuckoo sang from the unseen dark, and perfume of babla flowers came from the bend of the road.
>
> I stood speechless with shame when my name thou didst ask. Indeed, what had I done for thee to keep me in remembrance? But the memory that I could give water to thee to allay thy thirst will cling to my heart and enfold it in sweetness. The morning hour is late, the bird sings in weary notes, neem leaves rustle overhead and I sit and think and think.[58]

Rabindranath Tagore follows the tradition of natural, spontaneous devotion (*Sahaj Shakti*) of the Vaishnava poets. The core of the Vaishnav poetry is the natural, spontaneous expression of the devotee's love for the Eternal Lover, and the Vaishnava poets unmistakably believe that the senses lead the devotee to the celestial joy. No wonder Rabindranath Tagore does not reject the joy acquired through the senses. This is evident from the following lines:

> No, I will never shut the doors of my senses. The delights of sight and hearing and touch will bear thy delight.
>
> Yes, all my illusions will burn into illumination of joy, and all my desires ripen into fruits of love.[59].

The Vaishnava poets stress that the spontaneous love of the devotee begets indivisible joy. Tagore expresses the same belief exquisitely in the following extract from *Gitanjali*:

> At last, when I woke from my slumber and opened my eyes, I saw thee standing by me, flooding my sleep with thy smile. How I had feared that the path was long and wearisome, and the struggle to reach thee was hard![60]

NOTES AND REFERENCES

1. Rabindranath Tagore, *Reminiscences*, p. 137.
2. *Ibid.*, pp. 74-5.
3. *Ibid.*, p. 138.
4. *Ibid.*, p. 139
5. *Ibid.*, p. 209.
6. *Ibid.*, p. 250.
7. *Gitagovinda of Jayadeva*: *Love Song of the Dark Lord*, ed. and trans. Barbara Stoler Miller (Delhi: Motilal Banarsidass, 1984), p. 79.
8. *Gitanjali*, p. 1.
9. *Ibid.*, pp. 63-4.
10. *Ibid.*, p. 64.
11. *Ibid.*, pp. 67-8.
12. *Ibid.*, pp. 47-8.
13. *Gitagovinda*, p. 72.
14. *Gitanjali*, p. 47.

15. *Ibid.*, p. 48.
16. *Ibid.*, pp. 37-8.
17. *Ibid.*, p. 44.
18. *Gitagovinda,* p. 82.
19. *Gitanjali,* p. 7.
20. *Gitagovinda,* p. 77.
21. *Gitanjali,* p. 63.
22. *Ibid.*, p. 37.
23. *Ibid.*, p. 1.
24. *Ibid.*, pp. 2-3.
25. *Ibid.*, p. 5.
26. *Gitagovinda,* p. 93.
27. *Gitanjali,* p. 19.
28. *Ibid.*, p. 37.
29. *Ibid.*, p. 16.
30. *Ibid.*, p. 63.
31. *Ibid.*, pp. 4-5.
32. *Gitagovinda,* pp. 92-3.
33. *Gitanjali,* p. 56,
34. *Ibid.*, pp. 7-8.
35. *Ibid.*, p. 26.
36. *Gitagovinda,* p. 97.
37. *Gitanjali,* p. 25.
38. *Ibid.*, pp. 15-6.
39. *Gitagovinda,* p. 96.
40. *Gitanjali,* pp. 8-9.

41. *Ibid.*, pp. 10-1.
42. *Ibid.*, p. 11.
43. *Gitagovinda,* p. 95.
44. *Gitanjali,* p. 22.
45. *Gitagovinda,* p. 87.
46. *Ibid.*, p. 125.
47. *Gitanjali,* p. 2.
48. *Ibid.*, pp. 67-8.
49. *Gitagovinda,* p. 97.
50. *Gitanjali,* p. 16.
51. *Gitagovinda,* p. 89.
52. *Ibid.*, p. 95.
53. *Ibid.*, p. 110.
54. *Gitanjali,* p. 65.
55. *Ibid.*, p. 63.
56. *Ibid.*, p. 38.
57. *Ibid.*, pp. 29-30.
58. *Ibid.*, pp. 35-6.
59. *Ibid.*, p. 49.
60. *Ibid.*, p. 30.

5

Persian Influence: Hafiz

India and Iran have been quite close culturally and philosophically since ages. It is an undeniable fact that the Persian Sufism and Persian arts have left a deep imprint on Indian thought, art and literature. No wonder Pandit Jawahar Lal Nehru asserts : "Among many peoples and races who have come in contact with and influenced India's life and culture, the oldest and most persistent have been the Iranians."[1] It is not surprising, then, if the myriad-minded Rabindranath Tagore, saturated in learning and knowledge of all kinds, came under the impact of Persian literature and art enriched by such intellectual luminaries as Firdowsi, Rumi, Khayyam, Sadi, Jami, Attr, Hafiz and others. However, it was Khwajeh Shamsud-Din Mohammed Hafiz, the apostle of all-embracing vision of life and lyrical appreciation of beauty, who fascinated Rabindranath right from his boyhood and shaped his mind and poetic art most of all the Persian thinkers and artists.

Though Hafiz (1325-1390) could not get the recognition he deserved in Iran, yet he was much admired in India even in the fourteenth century. He was invited to India by Mahmud Shah Bahmani of the Deccan sometime in the eighth decade of the fourteenth century. Then, he was extended invitation to India by another ruler named Sultan Ghiyathud-Din of Bengal. It was Hafiz who prepared a manuscript of the *Khamsa* of Amir Khusrow, the celebrated poet of India of the medieval age. Besides, Hafiz's son. Shah Nu'man, visited India and died at Burhanpur. All this goes to prove that Hafiz was quite popular in India, specially in Bengal, and exerted influence on Indian thought and poetry ever since the fourteenth century. It is a fact that in the nineteenth century Ram Mohan Roy and Maharshi Devendranath Tagore were known scholars of Persian language and literature. The Tagores, in particular, were deeply influenced by the Persian culture and art. They were fond of Persian dress, food habits, tastees, customs and names. Thus the various parts of their house were given Persian names, such as *'tosha-khana'*, *'dafter-khana'*, *'baithak-khana'*, etc.[2]

No doubt Tagore was born in a family given to Persian inclinations and tastes, but it was mainly his father who inculcated in him a special life-long interest in Persian thought, culture and literature. Persian language and literature constituted an essential part of the academic life of the family children and they were put under the care of tutors well-versed in Persian art and literature.[3] Naturally, Rabindranath Tagore took keen interest in Persian art and literature ever since his boyhood.[4]

Rabindranath's father, Devendranath, "possessed an excellent command of.. Persian."[5] and was extremely fond of Hafiz whose poetry would intexicate him during the moments of loneliness and mystic frenzy. Apropos of his fascination for Hafiz's poetry, and its magical effect on him, Maharshi Devendranath writes:

> At night I used to leave my bedroom windows open; and I enjoyed the cold night wind very much indeed. Wrapping myself in a blanket, and sitting up in bed oblivious of all else, I spent half the night reciting humns and the verses of Hafiz.[6]

During his last days, Rabindranath's father would invariably and repeatedly mutter and recite his favourite lines of Hafiz, quoted below:

> The bell is tolling. I have heard the call, and am ready to depart with all my luggage.[7]

Obviously, Rabindranath inherited his love for Hafiz from his father, and as in the case of his illustrious father, so for him also Hafiz became the favourite poet to whom he was deeply indebted in more ways than one. What is remarkable is the fact that his great love and admiration for, and gratitude to, the poet of Shiraz remained unchanged throughout his life. Thus it is not surprising that during his journey to Europe, he was "particularly drawn to Agha Khan, who read to him a great deal of Hafiz's poetry and discussed Sufism with him"[8] Later, in his old age when he was invited to Iran by Shah Reza Pahlavi, he could not say 'no' despite his ill-health and age, for, as he says, "how could he refuse an invitation from the land of his own and his father's favourite poets Hafiz and Sadi?"[9]

During his visit to Shiraj, the Shah presented him two scrolls with pictures of Hafiz and Sadi peeping from the heaven and rejoicing over the function organised in honour of Tagore. When he went near Hafiz's tomb to offer flowers in tribute, he stood motionless shutting his eyes for quite sometime and was completely lost in thoughts about Hafiz and his father. He recalled:

> How many couplets of Hafiz had he heard in his childhood from his father, and himself recited! Memories came back and the beat of the couplets echoed through his head.[10]

Tagore was given a copy of the *Diwan* (a collection of poems) of Hafiz by the Curator who asked the Indian poet to think of some wish with closed eyes and then open the *Diwan*. Rabindranath was told that at whatever page the *Diwan* was opened he would find his wish expressed together with the way of its fulfilment. Following the Curator, Tagore wished in his heart India's emancipation from the evil of religious bigotry and opened Hafiz's *Diwan* to read the following as is recorded by G.D. Khanolkar in his book on Tagore:

> Can there be any hope that the door of heaven shall open, and an answer be vouchasafed to life's thorny problems which torment us? Though the door stay shut for them who falsely arrogate to themselves the title of 'religious', yet be assured that to those who worship God sincerely, the door shall verily be opened.[11]

After this miraculous experience, Rabindranath sat before Hafiz's tomb in reverie for quite a long time, "Rejoicing in his sense of close kinship with Hafiz."[12]

The above description goes to prove that Rabindranath was profoundly influenced by Persian art and literature in general and by Hafiz in particular. What most fascinated him in Hafiz were the latter's *sufi* and hedonistic beliefs and doctrines. The rest of this chapter is devoted to a detailed discussion of the impact of Hafi's thoughts and beliefs on Rabindranath's mind and art with the help of apt illustrations from the works of both the authors.

Hafiz had a special liking for the particular type of Persian *Sufism* known as *Malamatiyeh.* The exponents of this philosophical school advertently aroused public derision and mockery against themselves. They did it deliberately so as to garb their worship of God and sincerity of love from the public eyes. There was yet another reason of their attitude of this type: it was their hatred for exhibitionism of spirituality and religious morality. The avoided mixing up with people, and held that the worldly attainments and honour were obstacles created by he Devil to restrain people from meeting God. Thus to them the display of devotion to God was abnoxious, for they believed that God, and not His creatures, recognised and reward their devotion, righteousness and piety. Obviously, their thoughts and way of life had little to do with social norms, likes and dislikes, and they did not hesitate in discarding the accepted morality and norms of life publicly. All this was bound to elicit the displeasure and condemnation of people, but these Sufis saw in it two-fold blessing; firstly, it inculcated in them detachment from the world which made it possible for them to devote themselves completely to God; and, secondly, it enabled them to curb the *sufi* self-pride.

Hafiz's unflinching belief in this variety of Persian *sufism* is unfailingly perceptible in many of his poetic compositions. Time and again, he can be seen assailing the pseudo *Sufis* and the religious or moral hypocrites, evincing his contempt for self-assumption and exhibitionism and this deliberately inviting social criticism. He is in convinced that a genuine lover of God cannot be harmed by public condemnation. On the other hand, it only helps him to intensify and purify his devotion to God. Hafiz affirms:

> I said " "They'll mock, if I go round thy lane." By God!
> no love escapes the mocker's bane.[13]

Hafiz, like the *Malamatiyeh Sufis*, firmly believes that public humiliation and ridicule are the fountain-head of dignity and honour for a true lover of God, and help him to attain his goal. Thus fear of social insult and shame are meaningless for him. He vociferously extols the *kalandar* for his unshakable trust in this type of *Sufism* in the following lines:

> Peace to that gentle kalandar who, faithful shown in all his ways,
>
> Said, e'en when wearing the zunnar, the chaplet of the Monarch's praise![14]

No wonder Hafiz cares a fig for the worldly achievements, fame and hounour. He writes:

The wise may deem me lost to shame, But no care
have I for renown or name.[15]

Rabindranath Tagore's poetry offers us numerous evidences of the influence of Rafiz's *Malamatiyeh* thought on him. This is evident in his delineation of the psychological reactions of the mystic to social indifference to, and contempt of, him. In this context, the following lines from *Gitanjali* are worth-quoting:

> Where dost thou stand behind them all, my lover, hiding thyself in the shadows? They push thee and pass thee by on the dusty road, taking thee for naught. I wait here weary hours spreading my offerings for thee, while passers-by come and take my flowers, one by one, and my basket is nearly empty.
>
> The morning time is past, and the noon. In the shade of evening my eyes are drowsy with sleep. Men going home glance at me and smile and fill me with shame. I sit like a beggar maid, drawing my skirt over my face, and when they ask me, what it is I want, I drop my eyes and answer them not.
>
> Oh, how, indeed, could I tell them that for thee I wait, and that thou hast promised to come. How could I utter for shame that I keep for my dowry this poverty. Ah, I hug this pride in the secret of my heart.[16]

Patently, the above extract has the echoes of Hafizian thought. Rabindranath's devotee-lover attempts to hide his real devotion to God and knowingly makes himself the object of public humiliation and ridicule. In this lyric, God is the lover and the poet is a flower-girl, the beloved. The flower-girl waits and waits for long and weary hours for her Divine Lover to come to her, but He does not come. Others come and pass by her, but He remains behind them all hidden in darkness. The flowers of love, which she has brought as her offering for the divine Lover, are taken away by others. Time passes on, evening comes, and the poor waiting girl is tired and drowsy. The passers by smile at her mockingly. She sits there like a beggar maid with her face covered with her skirt. She is unable to answer the questions of the passers by and she cannot tell them that she is waiting for her Divine Lower and that He has promised to come to her. She cannot tell them that she has no dowry for Him except her poverty. So, she keeps silence and proudly keeps her secret to herself. The poor flower-firl sits and looks at the sky waiting for the splendour of His coming, for the time when He would come in His golden chariot with golden wings fluttering over it and filling the entire sky with golden light. He will descend and fill all with amazement by raising her from the dust and seating her by His side in His chariot. Trembling with shame and pride, she would cling to Him as does a tender creeper to the stout three when the wind blows. But time passes on and He does not come. Not even the sound of His chariot is heard. People come and go shouting with joy, but her lover still remains hidden in darkness. The beloved continuous to wait and weep, with her heart full of longing for the Divine.

Like Hafiz, Tagore holds that usually the mystic is severely criticised and insulted by the society, but he is not shaken and upset by all this. Nevertheless, an offence to his human self leads him to regard insult and condemnation as dignity, for it helps him to attain God. It is this attitude which imparts solace to his, converting his pain into pleasure. The second half of his beautiful lyric, cited below, fully brings it out:

> My companions laughed at me in scorn; they held their heads high and hurried on; they never looked back nor rested. They vanished in the distant blue haze. They crossed many meadows and hills, and passed through strange, far-away countries. All honour to you, heroic host of the interminable path! Mockery and reproach pricked me to rise, but found no response in me, I gave myself up for lost in the depth of a glad humiliation—in the shadow of a dim delight.

> The repose of the sun-embroidered green gloom slowly spread over my heart. I forgot for what I had travelled, and I surrendered my mind without struggle to the maze of shadows and songs.
>
> At last, when I woke from my slumber and opened my eyes, I saw thee standing by me, flooding my sleep with thy smile. How I had feared that the path was long and wearisome, and the struggle to reach thee was hard![17]

The above lines reveal the fact that the mystic has to tolerate the public ridicule and condemnation with the patience that distinguishes a *Malamatiyeh sufi*. He has to abandon wordly achievements which are the ultimate end of the lives of most of us, since he believes that it is a sure means of meeting the Eternal as is clear from the last line of the lyric.

Hafiz's view of predestination or choice of action shaped Tagore's mind to a great extent. There has been an unending discussion about this problem since ages, and yet no one universally-acknowledged theory has so far evolved. There are two contrary views about it: one is in favour of predestination, while the other rejects it. Those who support the doctrine of predestination believe that man's actions and their results are predetermined. God determines everything, including birth and death, and man is not granted the freedom of choice or will, and hence cannot be held responsible for whatever he does. On the other hand, those who discard this theory hold that man is not a puppet in the hands of God despite the fact that he has no control over birth, death, basic instincts, etc. Man enjoys freedom of will, and is endowed with the faculties of discretion, discrimination and conscience for treading on the right moral path if he so wishes. However, Hafiz believes in the middle course, neither supporting nor rejecting either of the ways completely. He thinks that man is a free moral being but his instinctual and physical aspects are predestined; he may not have absolute authority and freedom in all respects, but at the same time he is not completely a puppet in the hands of any agency, howsoever potent. Hafiz uses the word 'Kasb' for the man's ability to decide and act freely to a large extent, for his capacity to do or get something by his won efforts exclusively though even this power that man uses freely is the creation of God. No wonder the great Persian lyrical genius lays stress on human endeavour and action. At one place he writes:

> While life is thine, consent not Hafiz,
> That is should speed ignobly by;
> But strive thou to attain the object
> Of thy existence are thou die.[18]

Without work, nothing, in Hafiz's opinion, can be accomplished or attained. If man is not able to achieve anything, the cause is primarily inaction and his assignment of this reason or that for his having done nothing is not proper at all. As a matter of fact, the natural law of causation is fully operative in human life, and man reaps what he sows:

> How wisely to his son exclaimed the villager in years sunk deep;
>
> "Light of my eyes, as thou hast sown, expect thou at the end to reap"[19]

Thus in this world, man, according to Hafiz, is the architect of his own destiny to a large extent, and his misfortunes can be attributed to his indiscretion and limitless lust.

Naturally, God is not to be impeached for his ill-fate, but he himself is mainly responsible for it. The *sufi* of the type of Hafiz believes in his unconditional love for God and submits all that he does to Him.

It is not difficult to mark that Rabindranath has followed Hafiz in this respect. It is, therefore, not surprising if he has composed a full song such as this:

> 'Prisoner, tell me, who was it that bound you?'
>
> 'It was my master', said the prisoner. 'I thought I could outdo everybody in the world in wealth and power, and I amassed in my own treasure-house the money due to my king. When sleep overcame me I lay upon the bed that was for mylord, and on waking up I found I was a prisoner in my own treasure-house.'
>
> 'Prisoner, tell me, who was it that wrought this unbreakable chain?'
>
> 'It was I', said the prisoner, 'who forged this chain very carefully. I thought my invincible power would hold the world captive leaving me in a freedom undisturbed. Thus night and day I worked at the chain with huge fires and cruel hard strokes. When at last the work was done and the links were complete and unbreakable, I found that it held me in its grip.'[20]

The Prisoner of the above lyric appears to be the human incarnation of Hafiz's *Murghi hava gardan*, for he encounters his unfortunate end because of lust and indiscretion. Then, Hafiz's theory of Kash or resorting to action for achieving something finds a spontaneous expression in the following line of Tagore: "And it shall be my endeavour to reveal thee in my actions, knowing it is thy power gives me strength to act."[21]

Hafiz's poetical works evince his faith in pantheism or Non-dualism, that is, his belief in oneness between creatures. It is a well-known fact that the mystic beliefs in dualism or non-dualism are centred upon man's relationship with God or the communion of the Eternal with the temporal. The non-dualists place their trust in the fusion of their being with the Everlasting Being and proclaim that God is all. That is to say, they believe that the creator is synonymous with the creatures of the universe. On the contrary, the dualists are of the view that God and man are two entirely different entities, and the relationship between the two is based upon man's dependence on God. Undoubtedly, Hafiz goes deeper into the matter, widening the frontiers of the dualistic philosophy, by emphasizing the communion between human beings. Though the living human beings differ in outer form, yet they are similar as far as their substance is concerned. The communion between human beings has not only a material basis but also a spiritual one because all creatures have the same essence which is called the spirit or soul. However, it is not the same as the Absolute Being that the Pantheists believe in. Hafiz's Pantheism, i.e., his belief in the basic inner unity of creatures, finds lovely expression in the following lines:

> In Pahlavi his strain began the bulbul on the cypress spray,
> And in the mystic chant he sang at eventide of yesterday.
> H said: "Draw near, behold the rose has Moses' fire within her stirred.
> "To cause thee from the bush to hear the Unity's most subtle word"[22]

It was under the impact of Hafiz that Rabindranath Tagore developed a firm belief in the doctrine of phenomenal consubstantiality. The beautiful lyric of Tagore, cited below, fully evidences it:

> The same stream of life that runs though my veins night and day runs through the world and dances in rhythmic measures.
>
> It is the same life that shoots in joy through the dust of the earth in numberless blades of grass and breaks into tumultuous waves of leaves and flowers.
>
> It is the same life that is rocked in the ocean cradle of birth and of death, in ebb and in flow.
>
> I feel my limbs are made glorious by the touch of this world of life. And my pride is from the life-throb of ages dancing in my blood this moment.[23]

What is striking about the above song is that the unity of being of which Tagore speaks is not the *Vedantic* communion between human soul and God, but the fusion of the material and spiritual entities or man into the world surrounding him. Obviously, he was influenced by the poet of Shiraz in this respect.

Man's dependence on God, called *Tawakkol al Allah* in Persian, constitutes the core of his relationship with God according to the Islamic philosophy. This philosophical concept stresses that man must rely on God in all circumstances. It is only God whose kind help the *sufi* seeks during the hours of need because He alone is the true Friend and Saviour. Man's well-being and welfare wholly depend on God who is all grace and benevolence and who is the eternal owner and provider of all that exists in the universe, and hence is the only competent Person to help man and fulfil his needs and aspirations. Apropos of this, Hafiz writes:

> Aye gadayan-i-Kharabat Khuda yar-i-shuma-ast
> Cheshmi in'am nadarid zi an 'ami chand.[24]

Hafiz stresses that man's sole reliance on his own wisdom and ability amounts to infidelity. Despite his skill and discretion, he must depend on God's merciful competence to help him, for He is ever willing to assist and sustain His creation.

Rabindranath's poetry of the years of maturity often resounds with these ideas. A part of his lyric is quoted here in support of the above assertion:

> O Fool, to try to carry thyself upon thy own shoulders! O begger, to come to beg at thy own door!
>
> Leave all thy burdens on his hands who can bear all, and never look behind in regret.[25]

The capital letters in 'O Fool' evince the poet's emphasis

on the fact that it is a sheer folly of man if he depends on his skill and wisdom, and does not repose complete trust in God for doing or achieving anything in life because all men are imperfect and therefore can not help one another fully, while God alone is perfect and hence capable of doing anything flawlessly. In fact, man's highest wisdom lies in his absolute reliance on God in every matter, for only He is perfect and is the sole cause of everything, every matter and every creature. This is the reason why Tagore says:

> In the night of weariness let me give myself up to sleep without struggle, resting my trust upon thee.
>
> . . . .
>
> . . . .
>
> It is thou who drawest the veil of night upon the tired eyes of the day to renew its sight in a fresher gladness of awakening.[26]

The fundamental reason of Hafiz's severe, pungent attack on the religious and moral hypocrisy of his days is perhaps his whole-hearted dependence on God. He thinks that the religious and moral hypocrites care more for the gains from men, rather than for God. Their desire for material gains from men becomes a sort of veil which conceals the vision of God from them. The *Sufis* use the word *'Hejab'* for veil to symbolise all that misdirects man's attention from the One to the many, and muddles his vision of Him. They hold that the wrong attitude to religion and God hampers man's spiritual development. In Hafiz's opinion, it is this *Hejab* which is the primary cause of all religious fanaticism and dissension. Hafiz, as well as the *Sufis* of his type, believe that God Himself has put a screen on man's eyes in order to hide Himself till doomsday. The *Sufis* of the kind of Hafiz also hold that the Hejab is the result of man's immersion in this world and his fanaticism. Since the Hejab is man's own creation he can get rid of it by means of discipline and firm resolution. It is with these ideas in his mind that Hafiz condemns the so-called fake *Sufis* who proclaim themselves the seekers of God but are, in truth, completely given to the luxurious religion and the hypocritical morality. Criticising bitterly these religious frauds, Hafiz maintains that God can be attained by working hard like an humble former, and not by befooling the people through fake ritual activities.[27]

There is absolutely no doubt about the fact that Hafiz left an indelible imprint upon Tagore's mind even in this regard. The following song of *Gitanjali* can be quoted to illustrate the point:

> Leave this chanting and singing and telling of beads! Whom dost thou worship in this lonely dark corner of a temple with doors all shut? Open thine eyes and see thy God is not before thee!
>
> He is there where the tiller is tilling the hard ground and where the pathmaker is breaking stones. He is with them in sun and in shower, and his garment is covered with dust. Put off thy holy mantle and even like him come down on the dusty soil!
>
> ....
>
> ....
>
> Come out of thy meditation and leave aside thy flowers and incense ! What harm is there if thy clothes become tattered and stained? Meet him and stand by him in toil and in sweat of thy brow.[28]

The mystics and *sufis* think that God cannot be seen by man through his physical eyes, but His presence and nearness can unmistakably be felt by him through his unveiled inward eyes. The worldliness puts a thick mist on man's vision of God, and the dust of the earthly desires completely blurs this vision. Naturally, the sooner the mist and dust of earthliness are brushed away, the clearer becomes the vision of God and the happier is the man who does it. In the words of Hafiz:

> Void of veil and curtain is the Loved One's mien:
> Lay the dust and clearly is His beauty seen.[29]

Thus, man, according to Hafiz, is to be blamed for depriving his consciousness of the Divine Presence, for it is his importance to his own self that casts a veil on his inward eye through which alone he can realise His nearness. Just as man cannot see both the sky and the earth at one and the same time, so he can not have the vision of God without the adequate use of his inner eye. It is only when the curtain is removed from his inner eye that man can see Him face to face, and can experience bliss and true serenity.

Rabindranath Tagore was deeply influenced by these thoughts of Hafiz. The following lines of one of his sweet mystical lyrics bear witness to it:

> This screen that thou hast raised is painted with innumerable figures with the brush of the night and the day. Behind it thy seat is woven in wondrous mysteries of curves, casting away all barren lines of straightness.[30]

Again, in the Hafizian vein, Tagore has composed another beautiful song expressing his belief that man cannot have the glimpse of God till he acquires full control over his worldly aspirations and life of senses. To quote Tagore's own words:

> If it is not my portion to meet thee in this my life then let me ever fell that I have missed thy sight—let me not forget for a moment, let me carry the pangs of this sorrow in my dreams and in my wakeful hours.
>
> As my days pass in the crowded market of this world and my hands grow full with the daily profits, let me ever feel

> that I have gained nothing—let me not forget for a moment, let me carry the pangs of this sorrow in my dreams and in my wakeful hours.[31]

In fact, Tagore fully agrees with Hafiz by believing that the 'screen' or '*Hejab*', which is the creation of the physical plane of living, makes man incapable of feeling or seeing the Eternal Being. However, man is not able to shake off his awareness of Him completely, and hence he always awaits His arrival or presence before him. In this connection, the following lines from *Gitanjali* can be quoted:

> I have not seen his face, nor have I listened to his voice; only I have heard his gentle footsteps from the road before my house.[32]

Adhering to Persian *Sufism* in his own way, Hafiz feels that man is a pilgrim who endeavours to set aside all that obstructs his spiritual onward march. When he is able to get rid of worldly bondages, he reaches the stage of 'Void' or "Naught' for which the *Sufis* use the term 'La'. At this stage of his spiritual voyage, he becomes absolutely free from the sense of belonging to the world, the thirst for earthly gains and the sense of pride of this or that which never leave him even for a moment till he sets out the spiritual journey. Hafiz speaks of the stage of '*La*' or 'Void', which is possible only when man in an effort to merge into the Eternal Being is able to disengage himself from worldliness in these words:

> Thou who ne'r hast issued from the shrine of sense,
> How to Truths high pathway canst thou journey hence? [33]

To see and meet God, in Hafiz's opinion, man has to purge himself of all that is gross or impure in him. Just as a flower cannot grow on iron or zinc, likewise a man cannot see anything worthwhile, let alone God, in a mirror which is darkened by the earthly vapours. Inevitably, the purification of the inner as well as outer self is absolutely essential for acquiring the awareness of God. Hafiz puts this metaphorically thus:

> The benisons of Heaven are won by purity alone:
> Else, would not pearl and coral spring from every clod and stone?[34]

Man can do it only when he is preoccupied by God and nothing else. That is to say, he can accomplish it only by associating himself with Him, cutting himself off from everything else. Apropos of this, Hafiz writes:

> Hafiz his love-scroll
> To Thyself addressed,
> When he had cancelled
> What his heart loved best.[35]

The Persian poet wonders at the *Sufis* who assert that God dwellers in their hearts, for he thinks that their congested hearts cannot accommodate Him at all.

Since Hafiz's lyrics haunted Tagore's and his father's minds, it was but natural that again and again we find the echoes of his thoughts in his poetry. No wonder the above mentioned Hafizian thought finds an expression in one of his best-known lyrics, cited below:

> My song has put off her adornments. She has no pride of dress and decoration. Ornaments would mar our union; they would come between thee and me; their jingling would drown thy whispers.
>
> My poet's vanity dies in shame before thy sight. O master poet, I have sat down at thy feet. Only let me make my life simple and straight, like a flute of reed for thee to fill with music.[36]

Another beautiful example may be quoted from Rabindranath's poetry in support of the statement made above:

> The child who is decked with prince's robes and who has jewelled chains round his neck loses all pleasure in his play; his dress hampers him at everystep.[37]

Hafiz was not only a *sufi*, but also an epicurean. He resembles Omar Khayyam in asmuch as he is in favour of making the fullest use of the earthly existence. Thus, he may be called a mystic-materialist. It is not, therefore, surprising if many of his poems are soaked in epicureanism. Rejecting future pleasures advocated by religion, he often tends to be hedonistic. He firmly believes that "Deliverance" is not possible through the renunciation of worldly joys. Naturally, he pleads for enjoying the present life to the maximum possible. He avers:

> While sighs the saint for huris, and palaces above, The wine-house is my palace, the huri, one I love.
>
> Drain to the harp thy wine-cup; crush thus each woe that lives:
>
> And if they bid thee drink not, give answer: "God forgives."[38]

Obviously, heis not for holiness by means of penance and mortification. In fact, he pins his faith in the religion which does not favour the rejection of easy joys and 'dizzy raptures' of this temporal and spatial life. He is not prepared to give up the pleasures of sensuous life, the taste of red lips and the cups of wine. Just a couple of lines of one of his lyris sufficiently prove it:

> Why bid me, zealot, to Heaven's orchard rove?
> This chin's fair apple than that grove is better.[39]

Rabindranath Tagore's poetic mind was indubitably caught by Hafiz's epicurean trend of thought. The former's poetry and letters fully bring it out. In this context a part of his letter, written from Shelidah in October, 1891, can be quoted:

> I cannot make up my mind to sacrifies this precious gift of

> life in a self wrought famine, and disappoint the world and the hearts of men by fasts and meditations and constant argument. I count it enough to live and die as a man, loving and trusting the world, unable to look on it either as a delusion of the Creator or a snare of the Devil. It is not for me to strive to be wafted away into the airiness of an angel.[40]

Needless to assert, Rabindranath Tagore had a very strong penchant for the joys of life. This is the reason why even in *Gitanjali* which is universally considered as a collection of spiritual songs, he affirms:

> Deliverance is not for me in renunciation. I feel the embrace of freedom in a thousand bonds of delight.
>
> Thou ever pourest for me the fresh draught of thy wine of various colours and fragrance, filing this earthen vessel to the brim.
>
> ....
>
> ....
>
> No, I will never shut the doors of my senses. The delights of sight and hearing and touch will bear thy delight.
>
> Yes, all my illusions will burn into illumination of joy, and all my desires ripen into fruits of love.[41]

No wonder Rabindranath Tagore sets aside Buddhism, for the core of it is the renunciation of the world of senses. In one of his poems addressed to his friends, he maintains that he would never like to be an ascetic if it means the rejection of merriment and delights of life:

> No, my friends, I shall never be an ascetic, whatever you may say.
>
> I shall never be an ascetic if she does not take the vow with me.
>
> It is my firm resolve that if I cannot find a shady shelter and a companion for my penance, I shall never turn ascetic.
>
> No, my friends, I shall never leave my hearth and home,

and retire into the forest solitude, if rings no merry laughter in its echoing shade and if the end of no saffron mantle flutters in the wind; if its silence is not deepened by soft whispers.

I shall never be an asctic.[42]

It is to be observed that the reasons of Epicureanism in Hafiz and Tagore are almost identical. The former is quite logical about his pursuit for the principle of pleasure. He stresses that life is enigmatic and transitory and man cannot solve this riddle even with the help of the entire wisdom and learning existing in this world. Inevitably, man himself is the greatest enigma of this universe. Hafiz beautifully writes:

Bring wine, the ferry-boat to waft us o'er
This stream which laves an undiscovered shore.
Man is a riddle:

And but vain pretence
Is his, O Hafiz,
Who would solve its sense.[43]

The more the poet ponders over the world, the more convinced he becomes of the strange and mysterious ways dominating man's earthly existence. Thus wisdom and learning are of little value for solving the riddle of life, and the poets should not attach importance to them but should talk about wine and other such joyful things and matters. To quote Hafiz's own words:

Of minstrels and of wine discourse; care little how the skies revolve:

By wisdom no one has solved yet—and shall not this enigma solve.[44]

Life is not only enigmatic, but ephemeral also, and this greatly upsets Hafiz. It is short-lived, surrounded by death always. Death does not spare anyone or any thing and is a great 'leveller'; to it an idiot and the wise Aristotle are the same. This leads Hafiz to develop a deep love for the pleasures of life. There is irresistible joy in nature, which unmistakably gratifies man's senses, and this proves that pleasure is the law of nature, no matter the puritans and zealots my reject it completely. The recurring spring and the rejuvination of nature deepen man's biological urges and his desire for the 'aching joys' of life. But like beautiful physical objects of nature, the sensuous earthly pleasures are transitory, and therefore even the brief moments of these earthly joys are absolutely indispensable for man. In fact, a healthy heart is inalienable from the sensuous pleasures and natural urges of life. In the words of the Persian poet.

> As Hafiz, drain no goblet
> Unless the harp resound:
> To the silk string of pleasure
> The joyous heart is bound.[45]

Naturally, the hours of joy must be taken as the highest award, and man must make the best and the fullest use of them. This is why, addressing to himself, Hafiz says:

> A happy day, a time of mirth, a season for enjoying wine:
>
> Five days shall the occasion last—make it a prize, O heart, while thine.[46]

In support of his hedonistic attitude towards life, Hafiz refers to Adam, and points out that the first man in the universe, Adam, advocated the gratification of the senses, for the sake of which he did not mind his expulsion from paradise. The great Persian poet affirms:

> Strive always after ready bliss; for Adam, when by Fortune left,
>
> Abadoned the Abode of Peace, and of the Garden's joy was reft.[47]

He regrets that once he foolishly vowed not to kiss the lips of *Saki*[48] and not to taste the earthly and sensuous pleasures. Patently, he discards renunciation and penance, for these are not true to reason and are against the law of nature. Therefore, he avers:

> Come ! penance for a fair one's lips, and for the brimmer bright
>
> Is a wild freak which solid sense proves contrary to right.[49]

As a matter of fact, he is all for catching and enjoying every person or thing or opportunity that is enjoyable. This, according to him, is the panacea for all the ills, misfortunes and problems of life. This is the reason why he concludes one of his finest lyrics with these words:

> Hafiz, a medicine for thy woe,
> A medicine must thou sip,
> No other than that lip so sweet,
> That lip so sweet, that lip.[50]

This was the type of Hafiz's headonistic attitude towards life which enthralled Rabindranath Tagore's mind. Under the impact of this, his innate penachant for the beauty and joys of life deepened and found eloquent expression in his writings. No wonder he discarded asceticism and pinned his faith in aestheticism, in the principle of pleasures of life, and in the enjoyment of the moments of joy. Tagore's conviction that "this world is the world of wild storms kept tame with the music of beauty"[51] is Hafizian in its essence. Again, like Hafiz, he believes that life is transitory, that the lover and the beloved have a very brief existence, and that the movement of joy is as momentary as a dew drop. Thus he mournfully reflects after the sudden departure of his lady love:

> But ah, my evil fortune, time is short.
>
> Youth wanes year after year; the spring days are fugitive; the frail flowers die for nothing, and the wise man warns me that life is but a dewdrop on the lotus leaf.[52]

Obviously, he cannot afford to lose all that is readily available and to crave for that which is not easily attainable, for time and life flee fast.

Tagore demonstrates his belief in the acceptance of the world, asserting that the negation of it frustrates the very end of human existence on the earth. This explains why he hurries to pluck flowers lest they should be plundered by the passing winds, and why it "quickens our blood and brightens our eyes to snatch kisses that would vanish if we delayed."[53] As a matter of fact, he is of the view that every thing and every moment of this world must be enjoyed to the maximum. To quote his own words:

> Then, come, my rainy nights with pattering feet; smile, my golden autumn; come, careless April, scattering your kisses abroad. [54]

Rabindranath Tagore's *The Gardener* contains an exquisite song which has the reverberations of Hafizian belief in the instinctual basis of physical joys. The lady in the lyric is strongly opposed to the advances of her lover and to his attempt at kissing her, but when the jilted lover is gone, she cries in pain "why does he not come back"?[55] Rejecting the ascetic proposition, Tagore asserts that this earth is created by the same God Who has made heaven which is not beyond the 'rhythm of day and night' but is governed by the eternal principles of time and space. Furthermore, he affirms that heaven exists in sensitive human body and in palpitating human heart, and that

> Our life is short; it yields but a few days for love.
>
> Were it for work and drudgery it would be endlessly long.[56]

In fact, Rabindranath emphatically demonstrates his belief that the world is reality and is meant to be enjoyed. It is as lovely and attractive as the body of the beautiful beloved, though it is short-lived, full of' sound and fury' and restlessness. Thus, to him even the night of this world has a living, charming identity and is a definite source of joy. He writes:

> I feel thy beauty, dark night, like that of the loved Woman when she has put out the lamp.[57]

Like Hafiz, Tagore thinks that the world is transitory but pleasant, and that delightful objects, though meagre, are often easily attainable. Therefore, man's wisdom lies in his grabbing at these easily available pleasures, and not in trying to seek for the joys which might be achieved in future. The lines, cited below, clearly support the above assertion:

> Take to your bosom with a smile what is easy and simple and near. To-day is the festival of phantoms that know not when they die.[58]

Following Hafiz, Rabindranath is convinced that man must not miss the opportunity of enjoying a joyful moment even in the midst of grief and frustration. At times he appears to be as much of an aesthete and voluptuary as hafis is. It is, therefore, not surprising if he writes:

> It is heroic to hug one's sorrow ad determine not to be consoled.
>
> But a fresh face peeps across my door and raises its eyes to my eyes.
>
> I cannot but wipe away my tears and change the tune of my song.
>
> For time is short.[59]

Tagore, like Hafiz, feels that even Nature approves of the hedonistic view of like. This is evident in lyric twelve of *The Gardener* which is saturated with varied hedonistic joys in which Nature actively participates. In this song, the poet depicts the lake ripples clinging round the woman's feet and its waves jumping to kiss her neck. As a matter of fact, Tagore has composed numerous lyrics revealing his belief in the sensuous enjoyment of this world, caring little for the inner beauty and joy. Thus he writes:

> Be not concerned about her heart, my heart: be content if the music is true, though the words are not to be believed; enjoy the grace that dances like a lily on the rippling, deceiving surface, whatever may lie beneath.[60]

Tagore, like Hafiz, is fully conscious of the sensuous pleasures and is frequently thrilled by them. He feels that the mere touch of a woman's skirt results in the blowing of the warm breath of spring in his heart. Often he is completely over powered by the movement of joy, and under its magic sees everything else an illusion only. No wonder he sings:

> No mystery beyond the present;
> no striving for the impossible;
> no shadow behind the charm;
> no groping in the depth of the dark.[61]

Tagore, I these moments of 'dizzy raptures', rejects asceticism and the other-worldliness. He pleads for the present, the 'now', the moments of sensual excitement and unforgettable love-making. Apropos of this, he writes:

> Hands cling to hands and eyes linger on eyes: thus begins the record of our hearts.
>
> . . . .
>
> . . . .
>
> Your veil of the saffron colour makes my eyes drunk.
>
> The jasmine wreath that you wove me thrills to my heart like praise.
>
> It is a game of giving and withholding, revealing and screening again; some smiles and some little shyness, and some sweet useless struggles.[62]

The love between a man and a woman is the acme of worldly joy, and Tagore fully knows its value and accentuates it. Thus, he addresses his lady love with these words:

> The night has thrown up from its depth this little hour, that love my build a new world within these shut doors, to be lighted by this solitary lamp.
>
> We have for music but a single reed which our two pairs of lips must play on by turns—for crown, only one garland to bind my hair after I have put it on your forehead.
>
> Tearing the veil from my breast I shall make our bed on the floor; and one kiss and one sleep of delight shall fill our small boundless world.[63]

It is not surprising if in lyric eighty two of *The Gardener* he plays in the night the game of death with his bridge.[64]

Tagore's aesthetic and hedonistic attitude towards life leads him to ignore the scriptural prescription of the forest seclusion for man, i.e., *sanyas*. On the other hand, he believes that the forest hermitage is meant for the young, since the forest life abounds in the love-making of birds, bees, and flowers, and is the haunt of the young lovers' love-making. As a matter of fact, the old people should take charge of the household, while the youths live the life of forest-courtships and love-making. This is the reason why Tagore, like Hafiz, looks down upon the puritans, who detest the pleasures of life, by remarking:

> Reverend sir, forgive this pair of sinners. Spring winds to-day are blowing in wild eddies, driving dust and dead leaves away, and with them your lessons are all lost.
>
> Do not say, father, that life is a vanity.
>
> For we have made truce with death for once, and only for a few fragrant hours we two have been made immoral.[65]

Undoubtedly, Tagore follows Hafiz in his adherence to the principle of unreason. As has been pointed out earlier in this chapter, the Persian poet asserts that calculation or prudence cannot solve the riddle of life; on the contrary, it is only unreason that helps man to attain timeless serenity. Discarding reason, he says:

> As reason is a stubborn thing,
> Wine's cord, its neck to wring,
> Bring hither.[66]

Hafiz craves for wine and Saki in order to drown reason into the ocean of unreason, since this is the only possible way for the old and the young to experience joy in all its intensity in this world. He writes:

> Come hitcher, on the stream of wine let now my bark
> Be cast;
>
> Into the souls of old and young let riot's spark
> Be cast.[67]

That Rabindranath Tagore owes a lot to Haiz is explicit from the fact that he, too, laments his dependence on reason in the past and that he, like his illustrious predecessor, at last has to decide to rely only on unreason. The following lyric from *The Gardener* fully illustrates it and leaves no doubt in the mind of the reader about Hafiz's direct influence on Tagore's mind and art:

> O MAD, superbly drunk;
>
> If you kick open your doors and play the fool in public;
>
> If you empty your bag in a night, and snap your fingers at prudence;
>
> If you walk in curious paths and play with useless things;
>
> Reck not rhyme or reasons;
>
> If unfurling your sails before the storm you snap the rudder in two,
>
> Then I will follow you, comrade, and be drunken and go to the dogs.
>
> I have wasted my days and nights in the company of steady wise neighours.

Much knowing has turned my hair grey, and much watching has made my sight dim.

For years I have gathered and heaped up scraps and fragments of things:

Crush them and dance upon them, and scatter them all to the winds.

For I know 'tis the height of wisdom to be drunken and go to the dogs.

Let all crooked scruples vanish, let me hopelesslylose my way.

Let a gust of wild giddiness come and sweep me away from my anchors.

The world is peopled with worthies, and workers, useful and clever.

There are men who are easily first, and men who come decently after.

Let them be happy and prosper, and let me be foolishly futile.

For I know 'tis the end of all works to be drunken and go to the dogs.

I swear to surrender this moment all claims to the ranks of the decent.

I let go my pride of learning and judgement of right and of wrong.

I'll shatter memory's vessel, scattering the last drop of tears.

With the foam of the berry-red wine I will bathe and brighten my laughter.

The badge of the civil and staid I'll tear into shreads for the nonce.

I'll take the holy vow to be worthless, to be drunken and go to the dogs.[68]

The foregoing discussion fully brings out the truth

that Rabindranath Tagore and his father were fathomlessly fascinated by Hafiz, one of the greatest poets of the world of all times. Both the son and the father read and recited his poetry with immense joy. No doubt it was Rabindranath's father who created in him an imperishable interest in the Persian poet, but it was mainly his innate kinship with him that made him inseparable from him. Consequently, his entire being was saturated with the thoughts and predilections of Hafiz, and all this is plainly reflected in the ideas and attitudes embodied in the writings of this most renowned Indian poet of the modern age.

NOTES AND REFERENCES

1. Jawahar Lal Nehru, *The Discovery of India* (Calcutta: The Signet Press, 1946), p. 159.
2. Rabindranath Tagore, *My Boyhood Days*, trans. Marjorie Sykes (Calcutta: Visva-Bharati 1986), p. 17.
3. Rabindranath Tagore, *Reminiscences*, p. 61.
4. *Ibid.*, p. 68.
5. G.D. Khanolkar, *The Lute and the Plough: A life of Rabindranath Tagore*, trans. Thomas Gay (Bombay: The Book Centre Private Ltd., 1963), p. 9.
6. Maharshi Devendranath Tagore, The Autobiography, trans. SatyendranathTagore and Indira Devi (London: Macmillan and Co. Limited, 1961), p. 250.
7. *Ibid.*, p. 27.
8. G.D. Khanolkar, The *Lute and the Plough: A Life of Rabindranath Tagore*, p. 235.
9. *Ibid.*, p. 319.
10. *Ibid.*, p. 321.
11. *Ibid.*
12. *Ibid.*

13. Herman Bicknell, *Hafiz of Shiraz: A Selection from his Poems* (Tehran: imperial Organisation for Social Services, 1976), p. 241.
14. *Ibid.*, p. 82.
15. *Ibid.*, p. 13.
16. *Gitanjali*, pp. 23-4.
17. *Ibid.*, pp. 29-30.
18. *Hafiz of Shiraz: A Selection from His Poems*, p. 39.
19. *Ibid.*, p. 254.
20. *Gitanjali*, p. 18.
21. *Ibid.*, p. 3.
22. *Hafiz of Shirag: A Selection from his poems*, p. 254.
23. *Gitanjali*, pp. 46-7.
24. *Diwan-I-Khwajeh Hafiz Shirazi*, ed. Syed Abul Kasim Injuyi Shirazi (Tehran: Sazman-i-intesharat-i-Javi dan, solar 1363), p. 65.
25. *Gitanjali*, pp. 5-6.
26. *Ibid.*, p. 15.
27. *Diwan-I-Khwajeh Hafiz Shirazi*, p. 187.
28. *Gitanjali*, pp. 6-7.
29. *Hafiz of Shiraz; A Selection from His Poems*, p. 115.
30. *Gitanjali*, p. 48.
31. *Ibid.*, pp. 52-3.
32. *Ibid.*, p. 8.
33. *Hafiz of Shiraz; A Selection from His Poems*, p. 115.
34. *Ibid.*, p. 131.
35. *Ibid.*, p. 130.
36. *Gitanjali*, pp. 4-5.

37. *Ibid.*, p. 5.

38. *Hafiz of Shiraz; A Selection from His Poems*, p. 162.

39. *Ibid.*, p. 249.

40. Rabindranath Tagore, *Glimpses of Bengal*, pp. 49-50

41. *Gitanjali*, p. 49.

42. Rabindranath Tagore, *The Gardener* (London: Macmillan & Co., 1966), p. 78.

43. *Hafiz of Shiraz: A Selection from His Poems*, p. 247.

44. *Ibid.*, p. 20.

45. *Ibid.*, p. 134.

46. *Ibid.*, p. 32.

47. *Ibid.*, p. 11.

48. *Ibid.*, p. 216

49. *Ibid.*, p. 197.

50. *Ibid.*, p. 178.

51. *Collected Poems and Plays of Rabindranath Tagore* (London: Macmillan & Co. Ltd., 1955), p. 312.

52. Rabindranath Tagore, *The Gardener*, p. 82.

53. *Ibid.*, p. 117.

54. *Ibid.*, pp. 82-3.

55. *Ibid.*, p. 67.

56. *Ibid.*, pp. 117-18.

57. *Collected Poems and Plays of Rabindranath Tagore*, p. 302

58. *The Gardener*, p. 81.

59. *Ibid.*, p. 83.

60. *Collected Poems and Plays of Rabindranath Tagore*, pp. 408-09.

61. The Gardener, p. 37.

62. *Ibid.*, p. 36.

63. *Collected Poems and Plays of Rabindranath Tagore,* p. 420.

64. *The Gardener,* pp. 140-41.

65. *Ibid.*, p. 79.

66. *Hafiz of Shiraj: A Selection from His Poems,* p. 163.

67. *Ibid.*, p. 168.

68. *The Gardener,* pp. 75-7.

6

Western Influences: Romantic Poets

Rabindranath's creative genius fully flowered under variegated influences of which the Western impact, particularly that of the Romantic poets, deserves special attention of any perceptive reader of critic of this celebrated Indian poet of global fame. In fact the atmosphere and surroundings in which he was born and brought up were charged with new concepts, many of which belonged to the West. His father and his relatives were the central figures of the modern Bengali world, fully conversant with the Eastern and Western thoughts, literatures and arts. It is, therefore, not surprising if the school course that he studied consisted of an all-round list of subjects, including Latin language and literature. It is well known now that in his tutorial work at home he was asked to render Shakespeare's *Macbeth* and Goldsmith's *The Vicar of the wakefield* into Bengali. His study of English literature, though unsystematic, was so extensive as there was hardly any significant work of it which he did not read closely right from the Anglo-Normal period to the 'thirties.

As early as 1878 Tagore published a critical essay on Anglo-Saxon poetry in the magazine called the Bharati. He read *Religion Medici* of Sir Thomas Browne with pleasure during his school days in England. He was familiar with Marlowe, and Edmund Spenser, and almost all of his biographers hold that he was very fond of Shakespeare. Of the writers of the Restoration period, he rated Milton very high. The precursors of the Romantic Revival, especially chatterton and Robert Burns fascinated him immensely. He translated several of Burns, and Thomas Moore's poems into Bengali. But the English Romantic poets of the early nineteenth century—Wordsworth, Coleridge, Byron, Shelley & Keats—strongly seized his imagination. He translated into Bengali two stanzas of Child Harold and several of Shelley's poems, including Epipsychidion, "Stanzas Written in Dejection Near Naples", "Love's philosophy," "The Wanderer", etc. Among the later nineteenth-century poets, he extolled and translated literary pieces of Robert Buchnan, Christina Rossetti, Mrs, Browning, Swinburne, Tennyson, Robert Browning, Edwin and Matthew Arnold. He brought out a brilliant essay on Oscar Wilde's *De Profundis* in the *Bharati*. Also he showed the excellences of authors like Myers, Webster, Hood and Marston to the readers of the *Bharati*. In addition, he cited some fifty lines of Iliad in his review of Meghanadbadh, and he wrote an essay on Dante and Beatrice in the *Bharati* of 1878 and rendered quite a good number of lines from *vita Nuova* and Divina Commedia into Bengali. The same year he brought out a short article entitled "Petrarch and Laura" and the translation of Petrarch's ten sonnets into Bengali. He was fully conversant with the nineteenth century European authors of eminence. He read, and wrote on Goethe and Heine of Germany, and Moliere, Victor Hugo, Gautier and St. Bernard of France. Inevitably, Tagore asserted that English education was of immeasurable value for an Indian intellectual, artist or poet:

> In fact, due to the influence of English education, suddenly a current of great change has burst into the calm and placid waters of Bengali society, some banks of this society are falling and others are being formed. The earth around some of the most deep rooted beliefs are being washed

> away and hundreds of new beliefs are taking new roots. When so much outside and inside us is falling topsy-turvy should we even then remain tied to the strings of ancient poetry, disregarding all sense of time and space. It would be extremely unnatural to expect that such a tremendous change would have no effect on our poetry.[1]

The numbers of the *Bharati* in 1881 brought out Rabindranath's writings of various kinds which unquestionably evince the impact of the West on him. "The True Spouse", containing his concept of love, is studded with illustrations from the works of Shelley, Arnold and Rossetti. To another issue of this magazine of that year, he contributed an article on Romantic melancholy and its deliberate demonstration by poets like Byron. Then come out his essay on the Romantic concept of imagination as the primary source of poetry with instances from English poetry. Also, he wrote a long essay on Oscar Wilde's *De Profundis*. Which he rated higher than Milton's *Paradise List*. The same year in the same magazine, the *Bharati*, he published his famous article entitled" Non-dualism and Modern English Poets", establishing that the pantheistic monism of Shelley, Arnold and Tennyson is, in its essence, *Vedantic*. In this very number appeared Tagore's short essay on the aesthetics of music based on Spenser's *The Origin and Foundation of Music*. During this period, the Western dramatic form, known as the Opera, inspired him to write Valmiki Pratibha. In the winter number of the Bharati of 1881, Rabindranath wrote on the origin of arts and referred to Matthew Arnold's Epilogues to define the nature of different fine arts: He made numerous statements about the merits of subjective and objective poetry, showing the superiority of the subjective poetry with the help of instances from English Romantic poets.

Despite his deep involvement in the national movement, and his active participation in the Indian National Congress in 1886 by composing and singing the opening song for it, he could not be blind to the Indian's indebtedness to the West. He proclaimed vociferously that any race indifferent to the illuminating Western culture would never be able to blossom fully. Thus in "New and Old", he voiced his belief in revitalising the Indian civilisation by adopting the best of the West without any reservation, for the very vitality of a living civilisation, inescapably depended on the 'give and take' of cultures. Though against the blind worship of the West, he put his point figuratively in the following words:

> Contemporary India has its ancient civilisation as a mine has its coal. When the law of give and take, growth and decay operated in it, it thrived as a great forest. There was the activity of spring and rain in it, and the natural growth of flower, blossom, and plant. Now that it does not change and growth has become superfluous. The light and heat of many ages is still latent in it but for us it is dark and cold. As we do not have the flame that can light it, we produce out of it only columns of pitch black smoke. What we collect by digging tunnels of research to this past is also useless—and even this natural wealth we are not collecting ourselves. All our coal comes from the Englishman's stores.[2]

The above discussion clearly reveals the fact that Rabindranath Tagore's creative genius grew under the potent impact of the West. He not only cited and referred to the Western writers in his writings time and again, but also directly admitted their influences on him. In the *Reminiscences* he confessed:

> Glancing back at the period of which I tell it strikes me that we had gained more of stimulation than of nourishment out of English literature. Our literary gods then were Shakespeare, Milton and Byron; and the quality in their work which stirred us most was strength of passion.
>
> . . . .
>
> . . . .

> There was another such day in English literature when the slow-measure of Pope's common time gave place to the dance-rhythm of the French revolution. This had Byron for its poet. And the impetuosity of his passion also moved our veiled heart-bride in the seclusion of her corner.
>
> . . . .
>
> . . . .
>
> Our minds from infancy to old age are being mouled by this English literature alone. But other literatures of Europe, both classical and modern, of which the art-form shows the well-nourished development due to a systematic cultivation of self-control, are not subjects of our study; and so, as it seems to me, we are yet unable to arrive at a correct perception of the true aim and method of literary work.[3]

All this leads us to infer that in Rabindranath's writing we are bound to find echoes of innumerable Western creative artists. No wonder Dr. Aronson affirms that "the poems of *Gitanjali* have been compared to the work of almost all the living or dead poets on earth, from Sappho to T.S. Eliot,"[4]

No doubt, Rabindranath's creative genuine flowered under variegated, countless Western influences, but what is most striking in this context is the fact that more than Shakespeare, Milton, the victorians or the great Greeks, he was influenced by the English Romantic poets. Wordsworth, Coleridge, Byron, Shelley and Keats were his models, and consciously and unconsciously they left their indelible stamp on whatever he wrote right from the beginning to the end of his illustrious artistic career. The indubitable impact of these great English poets of the early nineteenth century on Tagore can unmistakably be perceived in his concept of love, in his view of the True the Good and the Beautiful in his attitude towards Nature, and man etc as reflected in his writings.

The old Bengali love poetry before Tagore was preoccupied with the corporal aspect of love as against the abstract romantic infatuation. Naturally, the poets before Rabindranath were primarily concerned with the indirect depiction of the bodily charms of the beloved with the help of exquisite imagery. The repeated themes of their poetry were the tryst, the testing of emotions, the social attack on illicit love and the pangs of separation and neglect. Needless to say, the romantic ennui and the psychological complexity of modern love were unknown to them. They were concerned with simple emotions of love and unflinching faithfulness, and the pathos of the emotions painted by them emanated from the frustration caused by social restrictions and obstacles. Thus the old Bengali love poetry frequently describes the meeting of lovers against all kinds of odds, social, domestic and natural, fierce storms, fearful lightning, derisive peering eyes of the neighbours, and the frightening watchfulness of the family members are not able to stop them from meeting at a fixed place. Obviously, the element of love of this poetry is marked by fidelity social unacceptability, nobility of suffering and inherent instinctiveness.

The new generation of Bengali poets, including Rabindranath, was fully familiar with English poetry and found its visionary love immensely appealing. The new Bengali poetry was, thus, very much concerned with the love of the private world of imagination. Rabindranath, though deeply influenced by the old Vaishnava poetry, broke away from the conventional love poetry imbibing the spirit of English Romanticism. It is therefore, not surprising if he attacked the old concept of love and its Treatment in old Bengali and Indian poetry. Answering the charge of his contemporary critics that the concept of love in the new Bengali poetry was Western and not Indian, he remarked.

Does the writer mean to say that the same old Whispers,

> concealments, the hide and seek under the terrifying vigilance of the in-laws, the woes of separation amid sandal odours, the cuckoo (*kokil*) and the black bee (bhramar), the descriptions of the contours of the body with the recurrent references to Mount Sumeru should be continued as a poetic tradition. The contemporary poetry with open, fearless and liberalised emotions, free from the trammels of over-ornamentation and fierce, piratical emotions, should be eliminated because it is foreign. Which of the two is really harmful for us, the one that secretly sends poison into the veins or that which openly fights against society.[5]

Discarding outrightly the old view of love he explained the new one by stating that it was a brooding emotion which did not need an object to worship of pine for. Elucidating the new concept of love, which unmistakably showed the impact of English Romanticism, he affirmed:

> The love of our poets of olden days was too personal. That there could be love without doting on the hands, feet, face, eyes and nose, was beyond there imagination. They were bewitched by an individual, hence their fanatical idolatory. They were lit up with joy at a union of lovers and collapsed at their separation. They always sang in high notes, never sighed in the low key of melancholy.[6]

The new notion of love was, according to Rabindranath Tagore, characterised by softness and subtlety of feeling and instincts as against the harshness and loudness of passion and reality of the old love poetry.

Even some early poems of Tagore embody his new Romantic concept of love. The denial of the conventional love is apparent in *Evening Songs* in which pride, meeting and separation are relegated to a secondary place, while love as a means of infusing heart with youth and vitality is stressed. His sonnet entitled. "Manasi" cited below, fully brings out his highly imaginative attitude towards love, demonstrating has belief that the beauty of woman, the primary object of man's love, is the creation of man's heart and fancy:

You are not created only by the creator god O woman!
Man has moulded you transfusing comeliness
From his own heart, Devoted poets
Have woven your wear with golden yarns of imageries.
Endowed with a new glory
Your image has been made everlasting by the artist What
show of colours, what fragrance, what a variety of
adornments!
The pearls come from the seas and gold from the mines,

Heaps of flowers come from the spring-forest
Insects sacrifice their lives for colouring the feet.

Provided with very shame, decor an cover
You have been made rare and kept in seclusion.
Burning desire of man has fallen on you
Half of you is female, the other half is fancy's creation.[7]

The Romanticist, no matter he is a sensualist and an epicure like Byron, yearns for ideal love. The bodily pleasures are essential for him, but he is also concerned with ideal love. Thus, both the physical and the metaphysical sides of love fascinate the Romantic artist. Speaking of these two aspects of the Romantic notion of love Tagore remarks showing his deep interest in the bodily charms of woman:

> We always want some flesh and blood to fondle. Our heart like the skin of a rhinoceros, does not delight in a subtle and soft touch. We therefore, admire, Byron and the bodiless moonlike imagination Shelley is liked by few Bengalis.[8]

Evening Songs reveal his love for the physical being and also for something beyond it, while *Morning Songs* mainly embody the vision he had seen. *Songs and Sketches* deal with dream and reality with a stress on the former, while *Sharps and Flats* are primarily concerned with the charms of human body and the sensual side of love. Like a true Romanticist, he also sets out in search of a sacred spirit, who alone can satiate the need of his intense imagination.

He has before him the example of Byron who, though most earthly of all the Romantics, craved for an ideal woman of his imagination whom he could never find. Infact, in the Romantic love-poet, the inner vision supersedes the material world around him, the dream lover replaces the earthly one. This is the reason why a good number of Rabindranath's love poems are addressed to imaginary personifications, living in the world of effusive make-believe. The following lines can be quoted here to illustrate the point:

> By enfolding you in deepest embrace?
> Closest touches we shall exchange
> Engulfed in sweetest enchantment,
>
> On the door-steps of our two forms.
> Each day of my life would be tinged with your radiance
> unceasingly,
> Each night would be delicious with your grace.
>
> ....
> ....
>
> Is it a vainentreaty of desire,
> A deception of my fancy?
> Who has such a knowledge divine?
> Who can tell me with certain proof that in some
> previous life
> You were not a blossoming beauty in the bloom of love
> In a feminine form in the bower of my life?
> You remained my friend, in one place
> While you were in union with me:[9]

Rabindranath Tagore was deeply influenced by Shelley's belief in the 'Kindred Spirit' in whose search he might give his whole life. In Epipsychidion, the British Romantic poet describes this 'Kindred Spirit' as

> ... a being whom my spirit oft
> Met on its visioned wanderings, far aloft,
> In the clear golden prime of my youth's dawn,
> Upon the fairy isles of sunny lawn,

Amid the enchanted mountains, and the caves
Of divine sleep and on the air-like waves
Of wonder-level dream, whose tremulous floor
Paved her light steps;[10]

Likewise, Keats presents the vision of a youthful Diana in Endymion and of the beautiful faery-woman in "Lal Belle Dame Sans Merci". Rabindranath's essay, "True Spouse', which first appeared in the *Bharati*, no. 1288, was written under the impact of this idea of "kindred Spirit" of the English Romantic poets. The poem like "Unending Love" is also a poetic exposition of the same thought. The following extract from "Manas Sundari" can be cited in this context:

Guess, in what shape would it blossom in the eyes of a woman!
The shadow of eye-lashes so dense and long
And the glow of darkness of the eyes
Bring closer to the bewitched inner mind,
A night of blise.

Would your lips silent and immobile
Remain eager to part with nectar
Laden with the completest of messages!
in clusters of charm, how the body
Bursts forth in bud and then blossoms
to exult in irresistible beauty of youth un-endurable.
I know, my friend, for certain
If we chance to gaze upon each other
On a path of the life beyond,
We shall be taken aback,
The slumbering past would tremble with a start, on
awaking.

Those black eyes, I know, would peer into my mind
Full of everlasting congnisance
Like pole stars of my life eternal.
Deriving light from my eyes
And drawing desire from my soul,
My secret love has given shape to this face.
Would you took know me in your heart of hearts?
Shall we, both of us, ever unite?[11]

Shelley's idealisation of love had an irresistible appeal for Rabindranath Tagore. The physical and spiritual sides of love are exquisitely delineated at one and the same time after the style of Shelley in the following lyrical lines:

> I hold her hands and press her to my breast.
>
> I try to fill my arms with her loveliness, to plunder her sweet smile with kisses, to drink her dark glances with my eyes.
>
> Ah, but where is it? Who can strain the blue from the sky?
>
> I try to grasp the beauty; it eludes me, leaving only the body in my hands.
>
> Baffled and weary I come back,
>
> How can the body touch the flower which only the spirit may touch?[12]

Often Tagore's concept of love, like that of Shelley, shuns any loudness of feeling and any description of individual beauty. It becomes a kind of devotion to a perfect image. Tagore, in one of his essays, asserts that the poets "have to raise an imaginary idol of their love."[13] Naturally, we find the imaginary idol of love, the elusive presence of the personifications of this idealised love in many of his poems. *Evening Songs* abound in these personifications, and in this context poems like "Dedication", "Song Beginning" and "The Loss of Ego" are note-worthy. Again, the opening poem of *Songs and Sketches* is addressed to the dream-lover. Then the third poem of this collection is about the "unknown beloved." Her presence is also felt in the series of poems beginning with "The Memory's Idol". Like the Romantics, Rabindranath idealises woman, the object of man's ethereal love by presenting her as the very embodiment of the highest joy and beauty as envisaged by human mind during the most imaginative and dreamy moments. The lines, quoted below from the beautiful poem "Woman" fully illustrate it:

Nectar and Joy taking form in woman,
Have lifted restless waves to subdue
The male, proud in his isolation.
Behind the mystery of God's Tapasya
The sculptor seeks the pristine form in thought,
And has tried to capture in his own creation
This ephemeral beauty.

He has cast aside fear and shame,
The injunctions of the scriptures,
And made the Nude pure
Beyond the reaches of sensual pleasure.
The infinite pain in the heart of man
Thirsting for divine nectar in the earth's wine,
Scatters its trail
In song, canvas and stone,
Age after age, country after country,
Untouched by lagour,
Unsoiled by weakness,
One beholds her beauty
In the dream of the artist.[13]

Wistfulness and disenchantment are inalienable from intense love, howsoever ideal form it may assume. The long love poem entitled "Manas Sundari" is of special significance in this connection. It spontaneously expresses his concept of love characterised by idealisation, flights of imagination emotional fervour, intense longing and implict disillusionment. The very opening lines of this lovely long lyric fully bring out the point:

No work for the day!
Keep aside all rhyming poesy and song;
Come my dearest beauty, my muse, my vine of fancy,
The treasure for which I strove life long.

Just for once sit by my side.
Today is for our crooning and cooing,
Drinking in silence the golden wine of the glow of
dusk Until veins of the heart
Swell with the flow of radiant beauty,

Until the animation and bond of pain
Sunder from sheer ecstasy,[14]

Infact, "Manas Sundari" incarnates, in one single image all that the poet seeks—the spirit of poetry, the fairy companion of his chldhood, the partner of his past life and the eternal bride of the future. In its essence. It is a passionate expression of his fathomless love for beloved, imaginary or real. The poem embodies the consummation of love, bodily, imaginary, and spiritual all at once. The following extract is worth—quoting in this context:

Come my vision of loveliness, leaving aside the lyre,
Entwine your two bare hands round my neck, full of
embrace,
The touch, as of a lotus stem, gladdens the corners
Of my inner soul making the hairs shoot up;
Beating breast quivers, eyes moisten,
Bewitched body almost faints,
Only the heart flushes up to the very brink of my frame,
As if the bonds of the senses would sunder presently.
Spread half of your skirt
And make me sit with all care beside you.
Call me by the sweetest of endearing names,
Say "my beloved", say "my most beloved".
Reposing on my breast your face
Covered with dishevelled hair
Go on pouring into ears of my heart,
In lowest pitch aside, anything that occurs in your mind
Meaningless emotive words.

O my dearest, when I beseech you for a kiss,
Do not bend your neck smiling, do not turn your face,
Keep within the punch of your lips one complete kiss,
A radiant scarlet thrill of nectar for me, thy devoted
humble bee,[15]

Like Byron, Shelley and Keats, Rabindranath also craves for the complete immersion of the entire being—physical, mental and spiritual—in the love of the beloved and of the state of being absolutely free from the awareness of self of ego, Thus, he, addressing to the beloved, says:

Only cover my entire mind and body with your skirit.
Kidnap me from myself with all thy force.
With my bosom placed on thy naked breast,
Let me hear the mystery of your inner soul.
The tremors of your heart like fingers
Would strike the strings of my heart;
And waves of music would well up
Spreading over the length of life, a-quivering.

Let me not realise anything,
Let me say nothing,
Let me compose no songs,
Let me walk not over the path strewn with rhymes,
Rudely forcing the bashful heart to the outer-world.
I will tremble with the weight of music oblivious of the message.
I shall shiver and burn like a star in an unsteady glow.
I shall disintegrate like a wave towards, the wave that is you,
Either I shall live or die, I shall do nothing else.[16]

In the treatment of love Rabindranath is a greater escapist than Keats for he evadas a direct statement of personal love. His greatest poem on woman and love, "Urvast" embodies the unsophisticated intensity of emotion in an idealised and symbolic form. But since Romantic love in inescapably tinged by an innate frustation, a strain of sadness, Rabindranath's love poems often have the note of despondency, melancholy and discontentment. Love is not unforgettable, but it is fraught with pain and craving. Thus, in the memorable love poem "Shahjahan", the poet writes:

"... Where your pining love
Remains mingled
With the streak of ruddy dawn,
With the pitiful sign of the horizon of tired dusk,
With the disporting of the comeliness of formless Chameli in the full moon,

On the shore unkissed by words,
Wherefrom, the imploring eyes ever return touching the door-step.

This your radiant messenger for ages
Eluding the guards of
Time Travels silently with the message
"I have not forgotten, not forgotten,
I have not forgotten O my dearest."[17]

However painful love may be, the Romantic notion of it presents it is perennial, as eternal. This is the reason why in the poem entitled *"Tapobhanga"* Tagore asserts:

Cupid again and again
Is burnt to ashes by fire,
Only to be resurrected at last with redoubled brilliance.[18]

Like any great artist, Tagore was preoccupied with beauty but his obsession with beauty—physical, intellectual and spiritual—and his belief that it is inalienable from truth and joy unmistakably exhibit the impact of the English Romantics like Keats and Shelley on him. This is evident from the fact that in his lecture entitled. "The Sense of Beauty" he propounds his own concept of the kinship between beauty and truth with the help of the famous statements of the Romantic poets. In this connection, his remarks, quoted below, explicitly echo the ideas of the English Romantic poet, Keats who is perhaps the greatest worshipper of beauty in the realm of literature.

> All our literature, all our music and fine arts are tending towards the True, whether consciously or unconsciously; all of them seem to try to bring the True into prominent focus. The poet has said: Beauty is truth, truth beauty. The *Upanishads* too tell us: *Anandarupamrutam Yadvibhati*, all that is, is manifestation of his joy, His deathlessness. From the speck of dust at our feet to the stars in the heavens - all is a manifestation of truth and beauty, of joy and immortality.[19]

In fact, it is man's inborn sense of truth, which, according to Tagore, enables him to comprehand law in creation, and it is his innate grasp of beauty which makes him see harmony in the cosmos. Thus a great artist has a very strong sense of beauty and truth which leads him to realise the unification of beauty and truth, and this makes his work an expression of joy, truth, beauty and immorality. Apropos of this, Tagore states in the Keatsian vein:

> ... the more we comprehend the harmony in the physical world the more our life shares the gladness of creation, and our expression of beauty in art becomes more truly catholic. As we become conscious of the harmony in our soul, our apprehension of the blissfulness of the spirit of the world becomes universal, and the expression of beauty in our life moves in goodness and love towards the infinite. This is the ultimate object of our existence, that we must ever know that 'beauty is truth, truth beauty';[20]

Speaking of the close affinity of beauty in art with truth which is the result of the harmony between Man's Universe and the Universal Man, Tagore observes: "When our universe is in harmony with man, the eternal, we know it as truth, we feel it as beauty."[21] But the truth which art deals with must have a sensuous touch because it is only this kind of truth which is significant for the people of the world: "if there be some truth which has no sensuous or rational relation to the human mind it will ever remain as nothing so long as we remain human beings.[22]

Like Keats and other Romantics, Tagore can not conceive of a beautiful work of art alien to truth. In fact, man discovers his true self only in the realm of beauty and truth. The physical realities reveal, by contrast, the immensity of truth. Inevitably, man is not satisfied by mere facts; he is an inveterate seeker of truth that is inalienable from the beautiful. Therefore, it is not surprising if Tagore echoes the Romntics in his assertion about the function of art: "The building of man's own world, a living world of truth and beauty, is the function of Art. It is this that brings him towards the discipline of truth and the truth of his self-expression. All man's creative efforts stem from this search and discipline of self-realisation."[23]

Again like the English Romantics, particularly John Keats, Tagore affirms that art creates beauty born of not only the physical in man but also of the intellectual and spiritual insights, and hence it exercises immense influence on man. This leads him to believe that the good is beautiful, not because it is useful for us but because it is an absolutely integral essential part of life. Naturally, Beauty is apparent as soon as the Good and the True become one. About the Beauty born of the unity of the Good and the True, Tagore convincingly states:

> The Good is beautiful not because of its utility or because what it does to us. There is more in it than that. The Good, we say, is at one with the whole of existence and it finds a ready response in the heart of and whenever the Good and the True are in accord, Beauty stands revealed. Lakshmi, our Goddess of wealth, represents not only beauty and power, but also the spirit of goodness.[24]

Then, Tagore, like Keats, is of the view that beauty is much more than a mere necessity; it is a power, elevating us above selfish, narrow activities. Since beauty enables man to attain a higher state of renunciation rising above all kinds of smallness, there is absolutely no difference between goodness and it. Just as goodness reveals the glory of God in man, so beauty shows Him in all creations. Patently, goodness is beauty, or the two are only the two sides of the same substance, Apropos of this, Tagore writes:

> The beauty of goodness goes far, beyond what the eye can see or the mind know, it invests every thing with a little of God. It is because of its nearness that we often fail to see goodness as a form of beauty. But when we do, our

whole being overflows like a river in spate, and then we know that nothing in the world can be more beautiful.[25]

Undoubtedly Tagore's kinship with the English Romantics is evident from his belief in art as the embodiment of Truth, Beauty, Goodness and Joy. Since a work of art, according to him, springs from the deeply felt experiences, it incarnates joy which is eternal and hence inalienable from beauty. The highest good is truth, the unitary vision of which "brings both Joy and Beauty; the quintessence of Beauty."[26] Tagore avers that in the world of changing forms, this kind of Truth can be found only when the mind, is able to get ultimate peace and rest. Inevitably, the realisation of this truth leads to joy. This is possible only when truth is not known, but is felt by man as his own. In case we fail to experience joy in the True, it only implies that we have not felt the Truth as our own. "when we can see both the True and the Delightful in this way," remarks Tagore, "the realisation of the Truth and realisation of Beauty will be found to be one and the same.[27] He refers to Keats' oft-quoted line, 'Beauty is truth, truth beauty," to support his assertion.

Further, Tagore holds that Matter and Spirit are linked by beauty. Although matter is merely a mass or lump, but we get food and home though it. Naturally, it is absolutely indispenable for man, since we are bound to suffer immensely without it. In fact it is only through beauty that art gets rid of the gulf between Matter and Spirit brings the two close to each other, and this invariably results in joy. To quote Tagore's own words: "As soon as material objects are seen to be beautiful, they cease to be material. Sprit permeates Matter, while Matter in turn is vivified by the Spirit. This leads to joy."[28]

Wordsworth's conviction that joy is the fountain-head of all arts and Keats's belief in beauty as a perennial source of joy form the reframe of Tagore's expository and creative writings. Tagore repeatedly affirms that all artistic activities, whatsoever form they may take, are the natural expression of boundless joy. "The joy, which is without form," says he," must create, must translate itself into forms."[29] Patently, a song is an expression of the joy of a singer, a poem embodies the joy of the poet and so on and so forth. In short, "Man in his robe of a creator is ever creating forms, and they come out of his abounding joy."[30] This boundless joy which is the prime cause of all artistic acts and keep every person or thing alive, is not something very uncommon, it is quite common, since, as Tagore states, "Beauty is omnipresent therefore everything is capable of giving us joy.[31]

True, man's sense of joy, according to Tagore, "is the source and nature of the aesthetic being of man"[32], and it is art it is art which gives us this kind of higher joy through beauty. In fact, joy and beauty at a higher plane have no separate identity; they become one and are at the most only two sides of the same thing : "A thing of beauty is a joy for ever,"[33] to quote Keats's words. The artist grasps and experiences the principle of joy in all things, and communicates it to others. Since great art is primarily concerned with the Infinite in life and makes others apprehend it, it is always a source of ceaseless joy. This explains why even when the artistic activity is over and the artist is back to the world of sordid reality from the blissful realm of imagination, he is not separated from joy. Moreover, even a single work of art fills the artist with the type of joy the like of which he cannot derive from all the activities of his life put together. Apropos of this Tagore remarks; "The joy of art is in freedom to take a distant flight as fancy will; then, even after return within the prison-world, an echo lingers in the ear, as exaltation in the mind."[34] In this approach to joy and beauty in art Tagore inescapably shows the influence of Keats, wordsworth and other English Romantic poets of the nineteenth century.

If in his belief in the union of beauty and joy, Tagore echoes Keats whom he refers to time and again he also evinces Shelley's direct influence on him when he talks about the inevitable relationship between joy, truth and beauty. Tagore illustrates from Shelley's work his conviction that the artist's creative faculty approaches Truth only through its joy in creative activity.[35] Shelley, in Tagore's opinion, realised the vision of the Infinite in his perception of the Spirit of Beauty in his view of the world. The artist in man explicitly sees that creative act is reality, issuing from his belief in him and the Infinite that is creative. In this regard, Tagore observes:

> This great world, where it is a creation, an expression of the infinite—where its morning sings of joy to the newly awakened life, and its evening stars sing to the traveller, weary and worn, of the triumph of life in a new birth across death— has its call for us. The call has ever roused the creator in man, and urged him to reveal the truth, to reveal the Infinite in himself. It is ever claiming from us, in our own creations, co-operation with God, reminding us of our divine nature, which finds itself in freedom of spirit.[36]

In short, Tagore reterates his conviction in the trinity of Beauty, Truth and Joy as embodied in art. He also stresses that Joy, Beauty, Truth, Goodness and Power are mere synonyms; these are only the varied facets of one and the same reality. Needless to emphasise that in this kind of attitude to aesthetics, he unmistakably shows the influence of Keats and Shelley. When we read his statements on this subject, we are at once reminded of Keats's utterances like "A thing of beauty is a joy for ever", "The first in beauty is first in might," "Thou wast not born of death, immortal bird", etc. in addition to the one Tagore quotes several times, "Beauty is truth, truth beauty,"

Like Keats, Tagore has a passion for beauty which leads him to ecstasy. Thus it is not surprising if he setting aside day-to-day work and poetry and music, craves intensely for beauty at the very beginning of his famous poem, "Manas Sundari":

> No work for the day!
> Keep aside all rhyming poesy and song;
> Come my dearest beauty, my muse, my vine of fancy,
> The treasure for which I strove life long
> Just for once sit by my side.
> Today is for our crooning and cooing,
> Drinking in silence the golden wine of the glow of dust
> Until veins of the heart
> Swell with the flow of radiant beauty,
> Until the animation and bond of pain
> Sunder from sheer ecstasy.[37]

Tagore's exquisite long poem "Tapobhanga" is worth mentioning in this context. It is about the breaking of penance of Lord Siva, the one True Eternal, the embodement of Truth, Beauty, Joy, Goodness and the Eternal Time. The following extract from it fully brings out Tagore's unflinching faith in the unity of Beauty, Joy, Truth and Eternity:

> You yourself found out your profound beauty.
> Joyously you held out in your hand the lustrous vessel of nectar
> For the hunger of the universe.
> Intoxicated, as you danced that day from bower to bower
> In flashes, I composed my songs keeping the rhythm and beat of your dance
> Following you closely.
>
> With the beam of the moon on your brow
> And with the dream of Nandan in my eyes
> I glimpsed the sportive joy of the ever-new with all my heart
> I glimpsed the radiance of smile inlaid in comeliness
> I saw the hesitant gesture of joy of the blushing one
> The ripples of beauty.[38]

The long poem "Manas Sundari" is, like Shelley's "Hymn to Intellectual Beauty", an ode to Beauty in its universal aspect. Then, many of the lyrics of *Gitanjali* and *The Gardener* contain lines which again and again, display the poet's belief in the Beauty, inseparable from Truth, Joy and Goodness.

Rabindranath Tagore's lovely poem, "Urwashi" composed by the poet in quest for the eternal feminine, gives vent to his concept of beauty which has undoubtedly some affinities with Shelley's views on the subject as put forth in his "Hymn to Intellectual Beauty." The celebrated Indian poet refers to the Indian mythology of the churning of the ocean resulting in the emergence of two women—Urwashi, the very incarnation of pure beauty and love so ravishingly enchanting as to be capable of drawing and taming the heart of every man; and Laksmi, the very embodiment of Goodness and Beauty. Thus he speaks of the inseparableness of beauty, good, love and truth. In this context the following lines from this long poem, which is so rich in thought contents and expression that it is almost untranslatable, can be quoted:

> At the beginning of Creation
> Out of the churning of the ocean.
> Emerged two women—
> The one Urwashi, the peerless Beauty,
> The nymph of heaven,
> Queen in the realms of Desire,
> The other Lakshmi the Good,
> The Mother of the world,
> The Goddess enthroned in Heaven.
>
> Urwashi, filling the cup
> With the wine of fiery, boisterous spring,
> Steals the hearts of men
> Breaking their meditation,
> And scatters them wild
> Among the blossoming flowers
> And song of sleepless youth.[39]

Again, in the short lyric entitled "Woman", Tagore like Shelley and Keats, speaks of pure beauty existing in the dream of the artist beyond the reaches of sensual joys. Beauty of this kind is Joy itself and it is everlasting and good, and therefore called Nectar. In it the mind of man perceives the loveliness of the universe and forges the union of form and the Formless, thus transforming the ephemeral beauty into the eternal one. To quote the poet's own words:

Nectar and Joy taking form in Woman,
Have lifted restless waves to subdue
The male, proud in his isolation.
Behind the mystery of God's Tapasya
The sculptor seeks the pristine form in thought
And has tried to capture in his own creation
This ephemeral beauty. He has cast aside fear and shame,
The injunctions of the scriptures,
And made Nude pure
Beyond the reaches of sensual pleasure.

. . . .

. . . .

Age after age, country after country,
Untouched by languor,
Unsoiled by weakness,
One beholds her beauty
In the dream of the artist.
The mind of Man- banished from heaven
Draws to itself the Splendour of the Universe
And effects the union of
Form with the Formless! [40]

The philosophical lyric "I" is remarkable in that it expresses his profound belief that to the artist the beautiful is Truth as well as the Eternal 'I' through whom Joy can be experienced and attained. A few lines from this poem can be cited in this connection:

I turned to the rose and said: "Beautiful':
And it was beautiful.

You will say: "This is philosophy and not the poet's voice." I replay:

'It is truth, therefore poetry.'

. . . .

. . . .

In the workshop of this universal "I",
With brush in hand, colour on palette,
I found joy.[41]

Rabindranath Tagore's poem "Echo" also unmistakably echoes. Shelley's attitude towards beauty as presented in "Hymn to Intellectual Beauty." Explaining his view of beauty as enunciated poetically in "Echo", Tagores writes:

> The fact of the matter was that a longing had been born within my heart, and, unable to find any other name, I had called what I had desired an Echo. When from the original fount in the depths of the universe streams of melody are sent forth abroad, their echo is reflected into our heart from the faces of our beloved and other beauteous things around us. It must be as I suggested, this Echo which we love, and not the things themselves from which it happens to be reflected for that which one day we scarcedeing to glance at one another, the very thing which claims our whole devotion...This is the meaning of the longing which stire within us at the sight of Beauty. The stream which comes from the infinite and flows towards the finite—that is the True, the Good, it is subject to laws, definite in form. Its echo which returns towards the Infinite is Beauty and Joy which are difficult to touch or grasp and so make us besides ourselves. This is what I tried to say by way of parable or a song in the Echo.[42]

The above extract elucidates Tagore's concept of beauty as much as of Shelley's put in the following lines by the great English romantic poet:

The everlasting universe of things
Flows through the mind, and rolls its rapid waves

Now dark now glittering—now reflecting gloom—
Now lending splendour, wherefrom secret sprigs
The source of human thought its tribute brings
Of waters—with a sound half its own,
Such as a feeble brook will oft assume
In the wild woods, among the mountains lone,
Where waterfalls around it leap forever...[43]

Tagore's belief in the artist's sudden grasp of 'spiritual reality', forming his vision, has a close kinship with Wordsworth's vision of spiritual splendour. The ordinary, common things and experiences of life suddenly lead the artist to obliterate his self which generally colours everything surrounding him, and the moments of the annihilation of his self are the moments of unique experience or insight. Tagore illustrates it from his own experience as an artist. Like Wordsworth, he received directly a message of spiritual reality from a very simple, commonplace natural phenomenon. One fine morning he looked at the sun sedding its rays from behind the trees, and suddenly he felt a kind of mist disappearing before his eyes and perceived the morning light enveloping the entire world and laying bare "an inner radiance of joy.[44] It illumined his comprehension of life, and he began to see a great unity and meaning in all the things and facts of the world. In fact, he had the wonderful experience of spiritual illumination, enabling him to comprehend the essence of the reality of the universe and to look into the depths of things, to use the expression of William Wordsworth. The experience filled him with unending, Mysterious joy, and for many days in succession he found every person or thing, howsoever insignificant, clothed in profound meaning and joy. He had Wordsworth-like experience of living for some time in a 'self-forgetful state of bliss." When the new vision came to an end, a state of extreme uneasiness wrapped him. Speaking of his unexpected grasp of the vision of spiritual reality the commonplace objects of the world and its compulsion for expression, Tagore says:

> The invisible screen of the commonplace was removed from all things and all men, and their ultimate significance was intensified in my mind; and this is the definition of beauty.
>
> . . . .
>
> . . . .
>
> The poem I wrote on the first day of my surprise was named "The Awakening of the Waterfall". The waterfall, whose spirit lay dormant in its icebound isolation, was touched by the sun and, bursting in a cataract of freedom, it found its finality in an unending sacrifice, in a continual union with the sea. After four days the vision passed away, and the lid hung down upon my inner sight. In the dark, the world once again put on its disguise of the obscurity of an ordinary fact.[45]

Rabindranath Tagore points out that it is in this way that the celestial vision dawns upon the artist, and that after finding an expression in a work of art it melts away, leaving the artist's inner being again in the gloom of dullness of every day, commonplace experiences and occurrences. This is, in a way, an echo of Keats's following remark concluding his wonderful poem "To a Nightingable":

> Was it a vision, or a waking dream?
> Fled is that music; -- Do I wake or sleep?[46]

Tagore, like the English Romantics, holds that the artist grasps unexpectedly his vision, filling him with an irresistible urge for expression; it is a kind of sudden, subconscious recognition of something fundamental about life, some basic reality about the world. In this state, he becomes aware of 'a stirring of soul' within him, and discovers a wonderful 'unity of meaning' in his known world of experience. The condition of the artist during this process is, in Tagore's words, "like that which a man, groping through a fog without knowing his destination, might feel when he suddenly discovers that he stands before his own house.[47] These fleeting, transitory moments, revealing to the artist his vision, quite often, according to both Tagore and Wordsworth, proceed from apparently insignificant, commonplace things and happenings. No wonder Tagore in his childhood, usually full of the boredom of dull lessons of books, was all of a sudden thrilled to the innermost depths of his being by a simple rhymed sentence, "It rains, the leaves tremble." A new world with a profound meaning dawned upon him, overflowing his entire being with the creative urge for expression. He found everything in this universe in harmony with his being, and was overwhelmed with the unity of a vision; a resplendent unity of truth seemed to pervade the entire cosmos. The evanescent moments made him feel the presence of the Eternal Being in all his experiences and in the world around him. He saw the vision of this being uniting all things and expressing itself through them. About his comprehension of this creative vision of the artist, Tagore states, as Wordsworth does more times than once in his creative and expository writings, in these words:

> At once I came to a world wherein I recovered my full meaning. My mind touched the creative realm of expression,...The rhythmic picture of the tremulous leaves beaten by the rain opened before my mind the world which does not merely carry information, but a harmony with my being. The unmeaning fragments lost their individual isolation and my mind revelled in the unity of a vision. In a similar manner, on that morning in the village the facts of my life suddenly appeared to me in a luminous unity of truth. All things that had seemed like vagrant waves were revealed to my mind in relation to a boundless sea. I felt sure that some Being who comprehended me and my world was seeking his best expression in all my experiences, uniting them into an ever widening individuality which is a spiritual work of art.[48]

However, to have the artistic vision, the artist, Tagore rightly asserts, ought to be gifted with a keen sensitiveness which overwhelms his mind with the awareness of the natural and human world around him. This enables him to mark easily the 'miracles of beauty' in many of the everyday happenings. Thus Tagore, like the English Romantics and for that matter like any other great artist, endowed with a very strong sensitiveness right from his infancy, would occasionally come across the miracles of beauty in the day-to-day morning and evening sights and scenes watched by him in his childhood while walking in a small garden attached to his house. With the realisation of the vision. Tagore, like any other artist in general and like Wordsworth in particular, would feel "a larger meaning of my own self when the barrier vanished between me and what was beyond myself."[49] In a word, the artist is blessed with a sense of wonder, finally leading him to "the treasure house of mystery in the depth of existence."[50] Tagore undoubtedly owes considerably to William Wordsworth so far as his comprehension and enunciation of this concept of the artist's vision is concerned.

The influence of Wordsworth on Tagore is also visible in the latter's assertion that an artist must keep a distance from his artistic creation because this is the only way by which the subject matter cannot dominate the creative process and the created artistic work. A great work of art can be produced only when it passes through the mind of the artist, and is not created at the spur of the moment. The artist must maintain a distance from the man in him, and the creator in him must be all important during the act of creation. Apropos of this Tagore states:

> Not only in poetry, but in all art, the mind of the artist must attain a certain degree of aloofness—the creator within man must be allowed the sole control. It the subject matter gets the better of the creation, the result is a mere replica of the event, not a reflection of it through the artist's mind.[51]

Evidently, Tagore is very close to Wordsworth in his

attitude towards the process of artistic creation and clearly differs from Shelley. Wordsworth's view in this regard becomes clear when he defines poetry and speaks of its origin and creative process in the following words:

> I have said that poetry is the spontaneous overflow of powerful feelings; it takes its origin from emotion recollected in tranquility; the emotion is contemplated till, by a species of reaction, the transquility gradually disappears, and an emotion, kindred to that which was before the subject of contemplation, is gradually produced, and does itself actually exist in the mind. In this mood successful composition generally begins, and in a mood similar to this it is carried on.[52]

Closely allied to this is the fact that in his conviction and demonstration that the origin of art lies in man's emotional surplus, Tagore exhibits his indebtedness to William Wordsworth. His belief seems to have been founded on Wordsworth's theory of poetry as the "spontaneous overflow of powerful feelings," though he does not confess it anywhere. Speaking of art originating from the superfluous or surplus that is present in man's emotional relationship with the world, Tagore says

> Man has a fund of emotional energy which is not all occupied with his self-preservation. This surplus seeks its outlet in the creation of Art, for man's civilisation is built upon his surplus.[53]

Again, Tagore affirms that art has its origin in man's surplus emotionalism or felt experiences, and has little to do with mere utility which is limited and exhaustible:

> ...where there is an element of the superfluous in our heart's relationship with the world, Art has its birth. In other words, where our personality feels its wealth it breaks out in display. What we devour for ourselves is totally spent. What overflows our need becomes articulate. The stage of pure utility is like the state of heat which is dark. When it surpasses itself, it becomes white heat and then it is expressive.[54]

Tagore admits indirectly his debt to Shelley in his understanding of the fact that the realisation of the reality of the Eternal inhabiting the whole universe is the cause of the birth of all great arts. Tagore asserts that human spirit, and not science, can perceive the wonderful unity of relationship permeating the cosmos. It is man's primal imagination, fresh and immediate in its experiences, which alone can grasp the reality of the eternal Personality pervading the whole universe, and hence human personality too. All arts and creative activities are the result of the comprehension of this reality. In this context Tagore quotes Shelley's following famous lines from *Adonais*:

> That light whose smile kindles the universe,
> That beauty in which all things work and move.[55]

The British Romantic poets, particularly Wordsworth and Shelley, also influenced certain aspects of Tagore's concept of form. He opines that art embodies man's feelings in a form which is unique and individual but not abnormal. Tagore explains it with the help of Wordsworth's poetry. He cites the following two lines from the English poet's poem, "Why Art Thou Silent?" to demonstrate how the sentiments pertaining to a life deserted by love are embodies in a picture which is unexpected but moves every sensible reader with delight:

> ...a forsaken bird's nest filled with show
> Mid its own bush of leafless eglantine.[56]

As a contrast to these lines of Wordsworth, Tagore refers to some modern writings which he does not consider art, as they deliberately endeavour to cause shocks in the reader by overstressing abnormality just for the sake of creating an illusion of novelty and reality.

Then under the impact of Shelley, Tagore comes to grasp the fact that art does not permit rigidity of form and expression. If art does it, it degenerates and loses its real value. This is the reason why the metaphors, employed in art and literature, stimulate our imagination, and do not tame it. These metaphors, which symbolise our emotional perceptions, must inspire human mind to devise new possibilities of expression and metaphors, rather than to suppress and discard the fresh modes of communicating emotional perceptions. True, art should not degrade itself by using only the fixed laws of expression because in that case it drifts away from truth and beauty. Tagore illustrates it from Shelley's memorable poem, "To a Skylark" in these words:

> Shelley, in his poem on the skylark, pours out images which we value because they are only a few suggestions of the immeasurableness of our enjoyment. But if, because of their fitness and beauty, a law were passed that while thinking about a skylark these images should be treated as final and no others admitted, then Shelley's poem would at once become false; for its truth is in its fluidity, in its modesty, which tacitly admits that it has not the last word.[57]

Perhaps it is in the treatment of Nature and man that we can trace the impact of the English Romantics on Tagore most clearly. Though human beings, particularly artists have always been fascinated by Nature since that beginning of creation. But the distinction between the English Romantic poets of the nineteenth century and the pre-Romantic poets in regard to their attitudes towards Nature is very well-marked. The pre-Romantic poets dealt with Nature casually or used it simply for drawing images from it, but the Romantics delighted in observing natural scenery minutely and in painting word pictures of it as an end in itself. The Romantics were immersed in introspection and hence were capable of making the minute analysis of personal reactions to Nature. But for a highly subjective poetic outlook, a poem like Wordsworth's Excursion is impossible to conceive. The two attitudes towards Nature the ancient Indian and the modern European, particularly by the Romantic one of the nineteenth century English poets—are basically different from each other, and Rabindranath Tagore knew it fully well. While the former is intimate but casual appreciation of Nature, the latter is characterised by an emphatic, cultivated devotion to Nature. Tagore brings out the distinction between the two attitudes as follows:

> We fell we are one as a matter of course, we do not notice the ever changing variations of her moods. We live enveloped in a blind unconscious affection. The European approaches from outside, so his contact with nature is so pleasing, because he is able to maintain his separateness his union is so intense. He tries to win attention like that of a bride and nature also unfolds her peerless charms to capture his heart. He had known her as lifeless for long, with the emergence of youth he seems to have discovered at a glance her indescribable beauty and limitless charm, which we never discovered because we had never doubted it and never questioned it.[58]

Tagore thinks that the new European concept of Nature is more significant than the ancient Indian one, for the former is founded on "the spirituality of a union", while the latter is centred upon identification and intimacy.[59]

The naturalism of English Romantic poetry was a poetic creed, having the impact of contemporary philosophy. Also, it was shaped by some well-known Romantic attitudes of the time, such as the revolt against formalism and the philistinism of the city life, the love for the primitive, the quest for a living faith in consonance with the new developments in knowledge, etc. The English Romanticism of the early nineteenth century engendered and highlighted the highly imaginative view that an appealing landscape was an incarnation of the beauty and reality of life in the world. Its cardinal principle of the loveliness of Nature as a gift of God was not absolutely original because it was an integral part of all old religions directly or directly, but the dogma which it deduced from it -viz. an undefiled scenery invariably created a purifying effect on human morals and emotions—was undoubtedly new. Thus it drew the conclusion that wild nature always helped the proper growth of human personality and the artistic sensibility of a person, and it overwhelmed him with a sense of mystery and wonder leading his to a spiritual awakening and revelation. This naturalism cannot be called a religion in the strict sense of the term, but it certainly was cult according to which Nature was God and the Eternal manifested Himself in the various beautiful objects of Nature. Thus the theme of Nature became very popular in all the realms of art. Myra Reynolds Aptly observes in this connection:

> ...the change is a great one. From Pope to Wordsworth, from Le Notre to Repton from Kneller to Turner, from Richardson to Mrs. Radcliffe, from Brand Gilpin to Kent, the pendulum swings, Whether men painted pictures, or made gardens, or went on journeys, or told tales of love and adventure, or wrote poems, the new spirit was at work within them, sending them forth into the world of nature and biding them bear witness to her power and loveliness.[60]

In fact the Romanticist had a firm belief in the harmony and close relationship between Man and Nature, in the oneness between the two. Also, he was obsessed with pantheism leading him to transcendentalism. His belief in the benevolence of Nature filled him with optimism and progress of humanity too, that is, in millennium, in human society free from superstitions, tyranny, etc.

This new concept of Nature as an independent theme became first conspicuous in Bengali poetry in the second half of the nineteenth century with Viharilal as its Chief exponent. Rabindranath Tagore right from his poetic career was deeply influenced by the English Romantic naturalism directly as well as indirectly through Viharilal's nature poetry Admitting the impact of Viharilal's Romantic Naturalism on him, he writes: "The artless flute-strains of his lyrics awoke within me the music of fields and forestglades."[61] Then, at one place in his expository writings, he plainly points out that if he and Bengali poets like Viharilal had not been acquainted with English Romantic poetry, they would not have treated Nature in their poetry in the new fashion and that those who are not familiar with the nineteenth century English poetry cannot understand this new Naturalism in poetry even to-day.[62] No wonder even in one of his earliest poems, "Ban-phul" ('Wild flower') we mark the Romantic Naturalism in the exposition of the assertion that the city is the abode of evil, while peace and purity reside in natural objects. The poem begins with the assertion:

> I crave not for learning, nor
> Knowledge of man, of his world.
> I would rather be a wild flower
> That blossoms in the wood,
> And withers there.

The heroine of this poetical piece suffers terribly from the wounds inflicted on her by the so-called civilised world, but she is convinced that her wounds will be healed by her return to nature.

The long poem called Kavikahini ("The Poet's Story"), which appeared in the first volume of his published poetry, further brings out Tagore's Romantic concept of Nature. The poem also clearly shows the influence of Wordsworth and Shelley on him. Shelley's Alastor and Wordsworth's Excursion made him believe that his poetic soul could feel satisfied not through fulfilment in love but by his return to Nature. His worship of Nature is as genuine as that of Wordsworth's or Shelleys. The following extract evidences it:

> Mother Nature, to pursue thy truth
> To the farthest end with the faltering wit of man
> By your grace, have I sought that far
> And shall ever seek.[63]

Another notable nature poem of the earliest phase of Tagore's poetic career is *"Phul bala* "(Flower Maiden). It is rich in Romantic love for garden, trees, creepers, bushes, etc. *Saisab Sangit,* his memorable juvenile verses, abound in poetic pieces saturated with ardent love for nature. At the age of eighteen, he composed a poem named *"Bhagna Hriday"* ("The Broken Heart"), which, though not essentially a nature poem, is studded with lines such as these:

> Then Mother Nature would herself teach
> The tale of Time.
> My heart, a wistful nursling at her breast,
> Would be filled with joyous harmonies.[64]

The above references to his early poetry go to prove that Tagore was an ardent lover of Nature like Wordsworth and other Romantics right from his childhood. About this, he also states in Reminiscences, the memory pictures of his inner life:

> From my earliest years I enjoyed a simple and intimate communion with Nature. Each one of the cocoanut trees in our garden had for me a distinct personality. When, on coming home from the Normal School, I saw behindthe sky-line of our roof-terrace blue-grey, water-laden clouds thickly banked up, the immense depth of gladness which filled me, all in a moment, I can recall clearly even now. On opening my eyes every morning, the blithely awakening world used to call me to join it like a playmate; the perfervid noonday sky, during the long silent watches of the siesta hours, would spirit me away from the workaday world into the recesses of its hermit cell; and the darkness of night would open the door to its phantom paths, and take me over all the seven seas and thirteen rivers, past all possibilities and impossibilities, right into its wonderland.[65]

Apparently, Tagore's Romantic Naturalism not only reveals the impact of the English Romantics on him but also his innate kinship with them.

It was during this period of his literary life that Tagore became fully conscious of Romantic Naturalism. Thus, in one of the critical pieces he published in the magazine *The Bharati*, he points out, in detail, how the Bengali poetry upto his times is miserably lacking in the treatment of Nature of the type we come across in the English Romantic poetry. He proves by illustrations how in Bengali poetry the description of a garden by one poet is repeated by another. To show how in the treatment of Nature English Romantic poetry is simply wonderful and unique in comparison with Bengali poetry, he quotes Shelley's description of the Ionian Island in Epipsychidion. Then he refers to the two stanzas from "The Sensitve Plant" by Shelley to say, "How many of us can realise the timid beauty of an occurrence such as the blossoming of the narcissus by the brook, or the withering of the rose, petal by petal. But look at our standards! Do we need imagination for such as these...To see these the heart and soul of a thing, is the highest function of observation. In the descriptions of nature in Bengali poetry these are missing."[66]

Rabindranath's first significant poetical work entitled The Evening Songs marks a change in his attitude towards Nature in that Nature forms one of the main themes and even though it is not the main theme of this work it is not eclipsed by the dominant strain of erotic melancholy. As a matter of fact, the poet finds Nature inseparable from his poetry. It is the refuge for his lovers, and they enjoy only the company of 'the soft-hearted breeze', 'the winds' and 'the dawn', and the tone of the poet in these poems reminds the reader of Keats's famous ulterance: "The roaring wind is my wife, and the stars through the window-pane my children."

The next poetical work, *The Morning Songs*, brings to light Tagore's further growth as a poet of Nature, presenting a scientific attitude towards it. He shows the world issuing from the sun as a fountain of fire, very much like the

Ganges streaming down from the head of Lord Siva. In fact, these poems describe vividly the scientific sources of all the natural phenomena, very much in the same way as Shelley does in poems like "The cloud", etc. In every : flower in blossom' and in 'every bird on its wing', the poet perceives

> Life astir and aflow every where,
> An endless unfolding of the world.

The poem, "Ekakini" ("The Lonely") evidences the impact of Wordsworth's "The Solitary Reaper" on Tagore and fully establishes his reputation as an outstanding Bengali poet steeped in Romantic Naturalism. In fact, at this stage of his poetic career, natural scenes and sights would impart him unique visions and insights as it was in the case of Wordsworth. In support of this, one of the many memories recorded by him can be quoted below just to stress the fact that he was greatly influenced by Wordsworth in his concept of Nature:

> One day, late in the afternoon, I was pacing the terrace of our Jorasanko house. The afterglow of the sunset combined with the wan twilight in a way which seemed to give the appoaching evening a specially wonderful attractiveness for me. Even the walls of the adjoining house seemed to grow beautiful. Is this uplifting of the cover of triviality from the everyday world, I wondered, due to some magic in the evening light? Never!
>
> I could see at once that it was the effect of the evening which had come within me; its shades had obliterated my self. While the self was rampant during the glare of day, everything I perceived was mingled with and hidden by it, Now that the self was put into the background, I could see the world in its own true aspect. And that aspect has nothing of triviality in it, it is full of beauty and joy.
>
> Since this experience I repeatedly tried the effect of deliberately suppressing my self and viewing the world as a mere spectator, and was invariably rewarded with a

> sense of special pleasure. I remember I tried also to explain to a relative how to see the world in its true light, and the incidental lightening of one's own sense of burden which follows such vision; but, as I believe, with no success.[67]

A little later, Tagore wrote a dramatic poem, "*Prakritir pratishodha*" "(Nature's Revenge") The central idea of this work is a hermit's unsuccessful attempt at gaining a victory over nature by acquiring a true knowledge of self, setting aside all the laws of Nature and all the bonds of desires and affections. The poet could write this exquisite poetic piece because of the wonderful influence of natural scenes and sights of the lovely place Karwar where he composed it. The scenery at Karwar infused him with the realisation and conviction that the grandeur and splendour of Nature was not a fantastic creation of the imagination, but the very expression of the joy of the Infimate. About this he records in Reminiscences as follows:

> The sea beach of Karwar is certainly a fit place in which to realise that the beauty of Nature is not a mirage of the imagination, but reflects the joy of the Infinite and thus draws us to loss ourselves in it. Where the universe is expressing itself in the magic of its laws it may not be strange if we miss its infinitude; but where the heart gets into immediate touch with immensity in the beauty of the meanest of things, is any room left for argument?
>
> Nature took the Sanyasi to the presence of the Infinite, enthroned on the finite, by the pathway of the heart. In the Nature's Revenge there were shown on the one side the wayfarers and the villagers, content with their home-made triviality and unconscious of anything beyond; and on the other the Sanyasi busy casting away his all, and himself, into the self-evolved infinite of his imagination. When love bridged the gulf between the two, and the hermit and the house-holder met, the seeming triviality of the finite and the seeming emptiness of the infinite alike disappeared.

> This was to put in a slightly different form the story of my own experience, of the entrancing ray of light which found its way into the depths of the cave into which I had retired away from all touch with the outer world, and made me more fully one with Nature again. This Nature's Revenge may be looked upon as an introduction to the whole of my future literary work; or, rather this has been the subject on which all my writings have dwelt-the joy of attaining the Infinite within he finite.[68]

Obviously, Tagore attained perfect harmony with Nature, and since then was one with Her and the Infinte.

To Tagore, like the Romantics, the objects of Nature are living individuals and from their joyful life the poet has learnt the secret of joy. Several objects of the natural world in the rainy session thrill the poet with immense joy, and the poetic extract, quoted below, immediately reminds us of Wordsworth:

> The rains sweep the sky from end to end. In the wild wet wind the jasmines revel in their own perfume.
>
> There is a secret joy in the bosom of the night, it is the joy of the veiled sky in its hidden stars, the joy of the midnight forest in its hoarded bird-songs. Let me fill my heart with it and carry it in secret through the day.[69]

In this context, Tagore's beautiful lyric on Kalidas should also be referred to. The influence of Wordsworth on the poet is visible in as much as he affirms that even though Kalidas is dead and cannot sing the praises of the spring, the love-liness of the joyous season is bound to delight everyone, for the beauties of Nature are a source of eternal joy to mankind. To quote a few lines:

> Yet April carries the same flowers with which they decked their hair, and the same south breeze fluttered their veils as whispers over modern roses.
>
> And, to tell the truth, joys are not lacking to this spring, though Kalidas sing no more; and I know, if he can watch me from the Poets' Paradise, he has reasons to be envious.[70]

Wordsworth was essentially a poet of joy, and this distinguishing feature of his genius influenced Tagore greatly The Indian Romantic poet, like Wordsworth, realises that one moment of joy is eternity, and hence the entire universe is a play ground of joy. The temporal aspect of natural beauty is also the very incarnation of this spirit of joy permeating the entire cosmos. At least two poems of Balaka (Nos. 35 and 24) show that the beauty of Nature is an eternal source of joy; it is a joy which is a mystic revelation. The following extract from the former fully brings it out:

> When dew falls as tears from the morning sky,
> When riverside trees sparkle in sunlight,
> So close in my heart their shadows fall,
> Then I know.
> The Universe is a floating lotus
> In the holy lake of my mind.

Like Wordsworth, Tagore occasionally paints in his poems the "thrill of pleasure" of the animal world. In this, connection, one of his later poems written in old age, "Phakhir Bhoj" ("A Feast for the Birds"), is worth-mentioning. The poem is occasioned by the poet's joy at seeking a flight of birds fluttering and jostling for a feast of corn scattered for them. The joyous movements of the birds become to the poet that rich mine of ecstasy and wonder which become the very manifestation of the Eternal. To quote the very words of the poet:

> This is no restless flutter of a moment; it is the
> primitive story of countless ages.
> As through the dark holes of the lute the wind plays
> its music,
> So through the death-holes of Time's lute bursts the
> music of life, over which sparkles, all around, this
> endless theme of joy.
> It breaks, breaks at every step, but never dies.
> As light, streaming from some remote invisible centre,
> comes down in infinite forms and colours,

> So this bubbling joy of life is spread all over in sheer ecstasy. That perennial stream
> Nor stops, nor tires, age after age.
> That same ancient ineffable flashes before my eyes, in the dance of those milling birds.[71]

To Tagore as to Wordsworth, the Infinite, the all pervasive Joy and the lovely objects of Nature are one and the same. Thus at one place in the lyric entitled "Birthday" written by the poet on his birthday in May at an advancing age, Tagore affirms:

> I shall wander-
>
> Picking flowers scattered by the wanton wind,
> Gathering songs that float over birds 'nests' Awakened to life at the touch of light. This touch of the Universal Being, This joy of hidden life in earth, sky and water.[72]

Rabindranath shows his kinship with, and indebtedness to, the English Romantics, particularly Wordsworth, in his deep, genuine belief in the profoundly intimate, spiritual, relationship between, Nature and Man. He gives vent to his belief convincingly, and poetically in one of the letters quoted by Ajit Charavarty in his book on the poet in Bengali A part of the long extract is cited below:

> I can very well recall many ages ago the youthful earth just rising from her sea-bath to salute the new sun; at that moment I sprouted somewhere from its soil in the primal exultation of life, and blossomed as a tree. There was no animal life yet on earth; the vast ocean swayed day and night, and at times like a senseless mother smothered the little new-born earth in a mad caress. On that new soil I absorbed with all my limbs the first sunlight, swayed under the blue sky like a child blindly alive, grasping mother earth with the roots of my head sucking her breast. I flowered in a stupid joy and my new blossoms came....I have been born on the soil of this earth in each age Whenever I am face to face with her that perennial intimacy gradually rises in my mind.[73]

Inevitably. Rabindranath Tagore, time and again, ever since the period of maturity, has written poems about the inalienable relationship between human soul and the natural phenomena, howsoever sad or gay they may be. The following lines illustrate it fully well:

That is why on some days
When the autumn rays fall on the field
Golden with ripening ears of corn
Or when cocoanut leaves rustle in the breeze.
Glistening in the sun....

A great restlessness fills my heart.
Perchance memories come of the days
When my omnipresent soul
Pervaded the earth, the water
The leafy nest of the woodland
And the blue haze of the sky.[74]

The Romantics attached as much significance to Nature as to Man and this is also true of Rabindranath Tagore. The glory of Man was discovered in the Renaissance period—the age of the first flowering of Romanticism in England. The nineteenth century Romantic poets sang of the glory of Man. To illustrate it, a few lines may be quoted here from Wordsworth's *The Prelude*:

... In the midst stood Man,
Outwardly, Inwardly contemplated,
As, of all visible natures crown, though born
Of dust, and kindred to the worm; ....[75]

Elsewhere in the same great poetical work Wordsworth accentuates the inseparableness of human heart from the Eternal Spirit:

....whether we be young or old,
Our destiny, Our being's heart and home,
Is with infinitude, and only there; ...[76]

More than any of the Western poets of Man, Tagore

glorifies Man so much so that he proclaims that God is a beggar at Man's door and that He needs Man as much as the latter needs Him. The poem,"*Tumi Ami*" ("You and I") of Balaka expresses his firm belief that God needs Man for his fuller realisation of Himself:

> The day was when you were alone, when you knew not yourself.
> I come, and you woke up.
> And the whole horizon was lit up with dancing blossom of light.
> You made me bloom from flower to flower, and gave me the swing of forms infinite.
> You scattered me in joy from star to star, and took me back in your bosom again.
> You hid me in death to gain me back, in newer forms again and again.[77]

In deed, Tagore's endeavour to achieve a fusion of the love of God and the love of Man is Wordsworthian. Like the great English Romantic poet, Tagore believes that man's worship of God becomes meaningful only when he loves his fellow beings, howsoever humble and down trodden they may be, and when hard work becomes his motto of life. It is this faith in the nobleness of humble man and his humble deeds that gives birth to the following memorable lyric of *Gitanjali*:

> He (God) is there where the tiller is tilling the hard ground and where the pathmaker is breaking stones, He is with them in sun and in shower, and his garment is covered with dust. Put off thy holy mantle and even like him come down on the dusty soil!
>
> . . . .
> . . . .
>
> Come out of thy meditations and leave aside thy followers an incense! What harm is there if thy clothes become tattered and stained? Meet him and stand by him in toil and in sweat of thy brow.[78]

To Wordsworth, as well as to Tagore, Nature is the repository of the organic spirit which infuses in man a sense of belonging to the earth. In fact, in his mystical rendering of the transcendental unity, he again and again echoes the thoughts poetically expressed by Wordsworth. The lyric, cited below, is one of glaring instances out of many:

> How often, great Earth, have I felt my being yearn to flow over you sharing in the happiness of each green blade that raises its signal banner in answer to the backoning blue of the sky!
>
> I feel as if I had belonged to you ages before I was born. That is why, in the days when the autumn light shimmers on the mellowing ears of rice. I seem to remember a past when my mind was everywhere, and even to hear voices as of playfellows echoing from the remote and deeply veiled past.
>
> When, in the evening, the cattle return to their folds, raising dust from the meadow paths, as the moon rises higher than the smoke ascending from the village huts, I feel sad as for some great separation that happened in the first morning of existence.[79]

In his intensely strong plea for man's liberty and for the collective happiness and freedom of human face, Rabindranath Tagore evinces an affinity of spirit with Shelley and Byron. Like the Romantics, he is a staunch humanist, a true champion of the ideals of equality, liberty and fraternity. While he puts his resplendent vision of the world embedded in freedom, fearlessness, truth, wisdom unfeigned fellow feelings, etc. in these words:

> Where the mind is without fear and the head is held high;
> Where knowledge is free;
> Where the world has not been broken up into fragments by narrow domestic walls;
> Where words come out from the depth of truth;

Where tireless striving stretches its arms towards perfection;

Where the clear stream of reason has not lost its way into the dreary desert sand of dead habit;

Where the mind is led forward by thee into ever-widening thought and action—

Into that heaven of freedom, my Father, let my country awake.[80]

Tagore was immensely influenced by Shelley's *Prometheus Unbound*. Promethean courage, faith, hope and love form the core of Tagore's humanistic vision. Also, he frequently exhibits the Shelleyian prophetic fire. The poem, "Jhader Kheya" of Balaka, is replete with this fire in its rugged form, The poem fully shows Tagore the poet—Prophet of Shelley's brand, steeped in an unswerving faith in Man, Imparting a profound meaning to Promethean suffering. The humanist - Prophet is clearly visible in these lines of the poem:

All this blood-stream of the brave, all the scalding tears of a mother,
Shall they be lost in the dust?
Shall hot Heaven descent on a day?
Shall not the Lord pay back all this debt?
Shall not the night's penance wait for the break of dawn?[81]

Another poetic piece of *Balaka* entitled "Navavarser" is soaked in a vision of Man as eternal pilgrim, marching on towards the great Unknown with liberty, courage, defiance and detachment. The extract, quoted below, evidences it:

O Pilgrim, the dust of the rugged road is thy nurse:

Let thy garment of endless march wrap thee in its wind-swept folds.

Let it take thee away from life's fetters to horizons infinite.

The peals of the conch-shell-shall not sing blessings for thee;
Not for thee the soft trembling light of the evening lamp;
Not for thee thy beloved's tearful eyes.
Look at every turn of the crooked road, wait for thee
the terrible blessings of the evening storm the roll of thunder in the Sravana night.
On thy footsteps tread the greetings
of the deadly thorn the fierce fangs of the hooded serpent.
These the blessings for thee, O pilgrim,
the blessings of the Rudra.[82]

The above three extracts bring out the fact that Tagore was not merely a poet of the 'Ivory Towery. They show the agony of human soul. In fact, many of his poems breathe a note of defiance at the so-called usual victory of Evil over Good. His later poems in particular reflect his vision of

Man Supreme,

Man after God's heart.

The poet seems to believe that the creator, while creating Man, had the idea of Man as he wished him to be, and not what he is as a bundle of weaknesses. Like the English Romantics, he is an inveterate champion of Man in whom he sees the culmination of creation and the fulfilment of the creator. The concluding lines of one of his great later poems bear witness to it:

I have no caste,
May not chant the holy verses,
Beyond all temples' barriers
My worship is fulfilled today-
Coming from the realm of God,
Ending in the realm of Man;
Completed in the heavens in the illumined Being,
Completed in the closest joy in the heart of Man.[83]

NOTES AND REFERENCES

1. *Bharati,* No. 1289, p 259.
2. *Rabindra Rachanavali,* Vol. XI, p. 483.
3. *Reminiscencces,* pp. 181-184.
4. A Aronson, *Rabindranath Through Western Eyes* (Allahabad: Indian Press, 1934), p. 104.
5. *Bharati,* No. 1789, p. 259.
6. *Ibid.,* No. 1288, p. 79.
7. *Love Poems of Tagore,* Trans. Rabindra Nath Choudhury (Delhi: Orient Paper backs, 1983), pp. 15-16.
8. *Bharati,* No. 1287, p. 272.
9. *Love Poems of Tagore,* pp. 34-35.
10. *The Complete Poetical Works of Percy Byshe Shelley,* ed. Thomas Hutchinson (London: Oxford University Press, 1956), p. 416.
11. *Love Poems of Tagore,* pp. 32-33.
12. The Gardener, *Collected Poems and Plays of Rabindranath,* pp. 122-23.
13. "Woman", *Later Poems of Tagore,* Trans Aurobindo Bose (Delhi: Orient Paperback, 1984), p. 100.
14. *Love Poems of Tagore,* Trans. Rabindra Nath Choudhury, p. 17.
15. *Ibid.,* pp. 18-19.
16. *Ibid.,* pp. 26-27.
17. *Ibid.,* p. 100.
18. *Ibid.,* p. 150.
19. *Ibid.,* p. 17.
20. "Sense of Beauty", *Angel of Surplus,* Ed. Sisir Kumar Ghose (Calcutta: Visva-Bharati, 1978), p. 59.
21. "The Realisation of Beauty", *Sadhana* (Calcultta: Macmillan and Co. Limited, 1946), p. 141.
22. "Notes on the Nature of Reality," *The Religion of Man,* p. 222.
23. *Ibid.,* p. 225.

24. "The Real and the True," *Angel of Surplus*, p. 155.
25. "Sense of Beauty," *Angel of Surplus*, p. 56.
26. *Ibid.*, pp. 56-7.
27. *Ibid.*, p. 58.
28. *Ibid.*, p. 59.
29. "The Nexus of Beauty", *Angel of Surplus*, p. 67.
30. "Realisation in Love", *Sadhana*, p. 104.
31. *Ibid.*
32. "The Realisation of Beauty", *Sadhana*, p. 138.
33. "The Universal Literature", *Angle of Surplus*, p. 103.
34. John Keats, "Endymion", *The Complete Poetry and Selected Prose of John Keats*, ed., Harold E. Braggs, p. 65.
35. *Glimpses of Bengal*, p. 68.
36. "The Poet's Religion," *Creative Unity*, p. 21.
37. *Ibid.*, pp. 26-7.
38. "Tapobhanga", *Love Poems of Tagore*, Trans. Rabindra Nath Choudhury (Delhi: Orient Paperbacks, 1983), p. 146.
39. *A Flight of Swans* (John Murry, 1955), p. 23. (See Later Poems of Tagore, pp. 22-3.).
40. "Woman", Later *Poems of Tagore*, p. 100.
41. 'I (1)', *Later Poems of Tagore*, p. 90.
42. Rabindranath Tagore, *Reminiscences*, p. 225.
43. See Shelley's Rymn to Intellectual
44. "The Vision", *The Religion of Man*, p. 94.
45. *Ibid.*
46. *The Complete Poetry and Selected Prose of John Keats*, ed. Harold Edgar Briggs (New York: The Modern Library 1951), p. 293.
47. "The Vision", *The Religion of Man*, p. 95.
48. *Ibid.*, pp. 95-6.
49. *Ibid.*, p. 99.
50. *Ibid.*

51. "From Thoughts from Rabindranath Tagore", *A Tagore Reader*, p. 276
52. "Preface" to the Second Edition of *Lyrical Ballads the Poetical Works of Wordsowrth*, ed. Thomas Hutchinson (London: Oxford University Press, 1946), p. 938.
53. "What is Art?". *Personality*, p. 7.
54. *Ibid.*, pp. 29-30.
55. *The Complete Poetical Works of Percy Bysshe Shelley*, Ed. Thomas Hutchinson (New York: Oxford University Press, 1956), p. 443.
56. "From *'The Religion of an Artist'*, A Tagore Reader, p. 236.
57. "From *Thought Relics"*, A Tagore Reader, pp. 287-57.
58. *Rabindra Rachanavali*, Vol. II, pp. 556-57.
59. *Ibid.*, p. 557.
60. Myra Reynolds, *The Treatment of Nature in English Poetry* (Chicago, 1896), p. 327.
61. *Reminiscences*, p. 114.
62. *Rabindra Rachanavali*, Vol. II, p. 556.
63. *Rabindra Rachanavali*, Vol I (A) p. 11.
64. *Ibid.*, p. 488.
65. *Reminiscences*, pp. 226-27.
66. *The Bharati*, 1287, p. 259.
67. *Reminiscences*, pp. 216-17.
68. *Ibid.*, pp. 237-38.
69. Rabindranath Tagore, *Lover's Gift and Crossing* (Madras: Macmillan Pocket Tagore Edition, 1985), p. 66.
70. *The fugitive and Other Poems*, Collected Poems and Plays of Rabindranath Tagore (London: Macmillan & Co. Ltd., 1955), p. 408.
71. Quoted by S.B. Mukherji in "Tagore and the English Romantics", *Perspectives on Rabindranath Tagore*, ed. T.R. Sharma (Ghaziabad: Vimal Prakashan, 1986), p. 14.
72. *Later Poem of Tagore*, Trans. Aurobindo Bose (Delhi: Orient Paperbacks, 1974), .116.

73. Ajit Chakravarty, *Rabindranath* (Calcultta, 1366), pp. 50-1.

74. *Rabindra Rachnavali,* Vol. III, p. 137.

75. William Wordsworth, *The Prelude,* Book VIII, pp. 485-88.

76. *Ibid,* Selected Poetry, ed. Mark Van Doren, William Wordsworth: New York : The Modern Library, 1961) p. 311.

77. Trans. and quoted by S.B. Mukherji in "Tagore and the English Romantics, *Perspectives on Rabindranath Tagore,* ed. T.R. Sharma (Ghaziabad: Vimal Prakashan, 1986) p. 16.

78. *Gitanjali,* p. 7.

79. *The Fugitiva and Other Poems, Collected Poems and Plays of Rabindranath Tagore,* p. 431

80. *Gitanjali,* p. 20.

81. Translated and Quoted by S.B. Mukherji in "Tagore and the English Romantics", *Perspectives on Rabindranath Tagore,* p. 19.

82. *Ibid.,* p. 20.

83. *Later Poems of Tagore,* Trans. Aurobindo Bose, p. 64.

7

Summing Up

The present study is an attempt to scrutinise closely the creative and expository writings of Tagore and also the various studies made on him with a view to establishing the major influences which shaped the mind and art of this most celebrated Indian creative artist of the modern age. A great genius like that of his is essentially and fundamentally original and his writings are primarily founded on his initiative understanding and experiences of life and art; but it does not imply that he did not learn anything from his illustrious predecessors and contemporaries. The truth is that numerous Indian and foreign influences worked in his actively, and prominently contributed to the making of his art and ideas. He was fully conversant with, and equally at home among, the thinkers and writers of the East and the West. In fact, he belonged both to the East and the West, and he proclaimed it by remarking that his name 'Rabi', which meant the sun, fully explained it, because like the sun he rose in the East but travelled and belonged to the West as much. In one of his last poems written only a few months before his death, he admitted that his creative being got nourishment and life from numerous sources belonging to the East as well as to the West:

> My life is nourished by the river,
> And through its veins

> The gifts of many mountain peaks run down:
> Its fields grow richer from many rivers' silt!
> The wondrous sap of life
> Feeds the fields from many sources.
> Its dream and its awakening
> Are circled by many streams of songs
> That flow from East and West.[1]

The Tagore family formed the nucleus of the cultural life of Bengal of the later half of the nineteenth century and the early decades of the present century, and that it was proud of creating outstanding poets, artists, musicians and thinkers. Obviously, Rabindranath had art, literature and philosophy in his blood by birth as a result of being a member of this illustrious family. About the artistic environment of his home he writes:

> Most of the members of my family had some gift: some were artists, some poets, some musicians, and the atmosphere of our home was permeated with the spirit of creation.[2]

Right from his childhood he could get the opportunity of reading the classics of Medieval Bengali, Sanskrit and Western literatures under the supervision of competent private tutors.

The Bengal of Rabindranath's childhood was charged with new life, expressing itself in three great movements—religio-social, literary and national—all of which enriched, and in their turn were enriched by, Rabindranath's inborn genius. The religious movement was launched by Raja Ram Mohan Roy whom Tagore called "the great-hearted man of gigantic intelligence." The founder of the *Brahmo Samaj* or 'Theistic Church of India' based upon the teachings of the *Upanishads* and the believer in the harmony of all the great religions of the world, he exerted a very great influence on the thoughts and ideals of Tagore, who confessed his deep indebtedness to him in several of his addresses and writings. The literary movement of the age was initiated by the novelist Bankim Chandra Chatterjee who influenced a new life into the moribund Bengali literature by lending it a vision of beauty and fullness of strength. The National Movement primarily aimed at the rediscovery of the soul of India, the revival of her cultural past, and thus it was essentially a revolutionary movement and not a reactionary one. Aurobindo Bose, a close friend and disciple of Rabindranath Tagore, aptly sums up the powerful impact of the family and the provincial environment on the artist, overflowing him with inexhaustible creative urge and energy:

> In this challenging and invigorating environment the boy Rabindranath grew up, absorbing the music, drama and poetry that often filled the air of the great Tagore mansion, and here, while still in his teens, began his poetic apprenticeship. This atmosphere gave him above all the freedom to experiment, untrammelled by hide-bound literary conventions. He also read extensively and wrote on the literature both of his own country and of Europe. From now on until almost the end of his life, a steady stream of poetry, drama, short stories, novels, literary criticism, social and political essays, religious and philosophical discourses poured from his pen.[3]

There is absolutely no doubt about the fact that the main ground of Tagore's thoughts and art is Indian. Patently. He was influenced to the innermost of his being by the spiritual wisdom constained in the *Vedas* and the *Upanishads*. From these stupendous Hindu scriptures, he imbibed an undying faith in the Joy and Love of the Infinite permeating the entire universe. A perusal of the *Vedas*, particularly of the *Rig-veda*, infused him with the freshness of the early Aryan dawns, besides fathomless wisdom, The *Upanishads* also taught him that life should be lived as closely to Nature as possible, for this is the easiest way to hold communion with the Eternal and to fell His Joy, Love, Beauty, etc. This explains why he established Santiniketan. The morning and evening prayers performed at Santiniketan are essentially Vedic, bringing out Tagore's life-long, unfathomable interest in the ancient holy texts. The morning prayer is like this:

> Thou art our Father. Do Thou help us to know Thee as Father. We bow down to Thee. Do Thou never afflict us, O Father, by causing a separation between Thee and us. O Thou self-revealing One, O Thou Parent of the Universe, purge away the multitude of our sins, and send unto us whatever is good and noble. To thee, from Whom spring joy and goodness, nay, Who art all goodness Thyself, to Thee we bow down now and for ever.'[4]

The day at Santiniketan always ends with the following prayer:

> 'The Deity Who is in fire and water, nay, Who pervades the universe through and through, and makes His abode in tiny plants and towering forests—to such a Deity we bow down for ever and ever.'[5]

Thus, it is not surprising if many of his lyrics have a very close resemblance with the hymns of the *Vedas* and the *Upanishads*, both in thought-contents and form.

Perhaps no single person influened Tagore as much as Kabir did. He loved innumerable authors and translated their writings into Bengali or English, but he did not spend as much of his energy and time in reading, understanding and translating an author as he did in the case of Kabir. He rendered into English one hundred of his profoundly meaningful and significant compositions.

No wonder he contributed the most to the rehabilitation of Kabir to his rightful place in Indian literature and society by revealing to the world the real significance of his works. His moral courage and zeal for social reforms, his outright condemnation of rituals and caste-distinations his religion of love and his weighty mysticism fascinated and inspired Tagore throughout his life.

The *Vaishnava* poetry deeply affected Rabindranath in his youth, though he was fond of it even in his childhood, and it indubitably haunted him all through his life. The Banu Singha poems of his experimental period were, more or less, written in imitation of the vaishnava poets like Jayadeva, Vidyapati and Chandidas. Even later on, he wrote poetry after their style. For instance, in the "Golden Boat" he recognises, like the Vaishnava poets, the human becoming godly and the divine descending to earth. The poems like "You and I" and "Do Not Look So Humbly at Me" reverberate with the echoes of this highly emotional poetry couched in love. Even *Gitanjali* abounds in most of the salient features of the Vaishnava poetry. Pointing to the perennial charm and value of this poetry and its lasting impact on him, Tagore writes in *The Religion of Man*:

> Fortunately for me a collection of old lyrical poems composed by the poets of the Vaishnava sect came to my hand when I was young. I became aware of some underlying idea deep in the obvious meaning of these love poems. I felt the joy of an eplorer who suddenly discovers the key to the language lying hidden in the hieroglyphs which are beautiful in themselves. I was sure that these poets were speaking about the supreme Lover, whose touch we experience in all our relations of love - the love of nature's beauty, of the animal, the child, the comrade, the beloved, the love that illuminates our consciousness of reality. They sang of a love that ever flows through numerous obstacles between men and Man the Divine, the eternal relation which has the relationship of mutual dependence for a fulfilment that needs perfect union of individuals and the Universal.
>
> The Vaishnava poet sings of the Lover who has his flute which , with its different stops, gives out the varied notes of beauty and love that are in Nature and Man. These notes bring to us our message of invitation. They eternally urge us to come out from the seclusion of our self-centred life into the realm of love and truth..[6]

The Persian culture and art entered India and coloured her life much before Rabindranath was born. Thus with the beginning of his awareness of life, he was in close touch with the Persian mode of living and art because it was a part and parcel of the Tagore family. He came to know about Hafiz, an outstanding product of the Persian art and philosophy through his father who was very fond of this Persian philosopher-poet, early in his boyhood. No doubt he inherited his love for Hafiz from his father, Devendranath, but it was his innate kinship with the Persian artist that actually deepened his initial love for him into a life-long passion. Like Hafiz, he had an inborn craving for the Eternal, a deep aversion to the religious and moral hypocrisy of the people, and an abiding belief in the hedonistic attitude towards life which pleads for an instatable quest for the joys of life. Therefore, it is not surprising if Rabindranath's poetry, from the beginning to the end, bears the marks of Hafiz's dominant ideas and attitudes, and it may be stated here that the great Indian owes a good deal of his charm and appeal to the illustrious Persian man of letters. As a matter of fact, a close study of Hafiz's writings is necessary to understand Rabindranath's mind and art fully well.

Notwithstanding the fact that Tagore is out and out an Indian, the Western influences on him cannot be minimised. He visited the West a number of times right from his formative years. He could get education in England, travelled many parts of Europe and America, and read a lot of Western literature, both classical and modern, ever since his childhood. Naturally, it is impossible to analyse all the Western influences on him. But what can surely be established is the fact that his art and ideas were considerably shaped by the nineteenth-century English authors, particularly the Romantics. He refers to these authors repeatedly in his writings. It cannot be doubted that he was immensely influenced by Wordsworth's attitude towards joy and nature, Byron's revolutionary zeal, Shelley's concept of intellectual beauty and romantic melancholy and reformative fervour, Keats' cult of beauty and command of magnificient stanza forms, and Browning's psychological interest and his technique of telling the one story through different minds. But what particularly appealed to Tagore in these English poets was their wonderful power of creating their own individual universe which would, strangely enough, become the universe of the readers too. About this, he writes in his famous essay, "modern poetry", in these words:

> The English poets with whom we came into contact in my early youth saw the universe with their own eyes; it had become their personal property. Not only did their own imaginations, opinions and tastes humanise and intellectualise the universe, but they molded it according to their individual desires. The universe of Wordsworth was specially "Words worthian", of Shelley, "Shelleyan", of Byron, "Byronic. By creative magic it also became the reader's universe. The joy that we felt in the poet's world was the joy of enjoying the deight of a particular world aroma. The flower sent its invitation to the bee through a distinctive smell and colour and the note of invitation was sweet. The poet's invitation possessed a spontaneous charm. In the days when the chief bond between man and the universe was individuality, the personal touch in the invitation had to be fostered with care, a sort of competition had to be set up in dress and ornament and manners, in order to show oneself off to the best advantage.
>
> Thus, we find that in the beginning of the nineteenth century the tradition which held priority in the English poetry of the previous age had given place to self-expression.[7]

In conclusion, it may be said that like any great artist, highly sensitive and impressionable, Tagore was receptive to all kinds of impressions, ideas and influences. Moreover, he was a voracious reader, indefatigably perusing all that was available to him, old or new, Indian or foreign. Obviously, in his works we find the echoes of the ideas and art of numberless thinkers and artists of all kinds, and of all times and climes. Thus, it should not look absurd and amazing if scholars draw parallels between his masterpieces and those of the great artists of the world of all categories, such as the composers of the *vedic* literature, Kalidas, Vaishnava poets, Kabir, Hafiz, the great Greeks, Sappho, Shakespeare, Milton, Wordsworth, Byron, Shelley, Keats, Tennyson, Browning, Rossetti, Francis Thompson, Heine, Tolstoy, Dostoevsky, Walt Whitman, Kipling, W.B. Yeats, Ezra Pund, T.S. Elito and many others. But the truth is that he is not like this author or that, but is Rabindranath Tagore, who is strikingly unique and original in his own way in that in him all the best streams of thoughts merge into one losing their independent entities completely and are given a new colouring by his extraordinary innate genius.

NOTES AND REFERENCES

1. *Later Poems of Tagore,* trans. Aurobido Bose, p. 134.
2. "From My Life", *A Tagore Reader,* ed. Amiya Chakravarty, p. 84.
3. "Introduction," *Later Poems of Tagore,* p. 13.
4. Quoted by Edward J. Thompson in *Rabindranath Tagore: His Life and Work,* p. 77.
5. *Ibid.*
6. "The Vision", *The Religion of Man* pp. 105-6.
7. "Modern Poetry", *A Tagore Reader,* pp. 242-43.

Bibliography

I. English Translations of the Poems and Plays of Rabindranath Tagore

(a) Translations by the Poet Himself

Collected Poems and Plays of Rabindranath Tagore, London: Macmillan & Co. Ltd., 1955.

Fruit-Gathering. Madras : Macmillan Pocket Tagore Edition, 1985.

Gitanjali. Madras: Macmillan Pocket Tagore Edition, 1987.

Lover's Gift and Crossing. Madras: Macmillan Pocket Tagore Edition, 1985.

Poems, Calcutta: Visva-Bharati, 1942.

Stray Birds, London: Macmillan & Co., 1946.

The Crescent Moon, London: Macmillan & Co., 1961.

The Fugitive, London: Macmillan & Co., 1923.

The Gardener, London: Macmillan & Co., Limited, 1966.

(b) Translations of Tagore's Poems by Others

A Flight of Swans, Trans. Aurobindo Bose, London, John Murray, 1955.

Fifteen Longer Poems of Rabindranath Tagore, Trans. Rabindra Nath Choudhary, Bhubaneshwar: 125 Satyanagar, 1969.

Herald of Spring, Trans. Aurobindo Bose, London: John Murray, 1957.

Later Poems of Rabindranath Tagore, Trans. Aurobindo Bose, Delhi: Orient Paperbacks, 1984.

Love Poems of Tagore, Trans. Rabindra Nath Choudhury, Delhi: Orient Paperbacks, 1975.

One Hundred and One Poems by Rabindranath Tagore, Ed. Humayun Kabir, Bombay: Asia Publishing House, 1966.

Syamali, Trans. S. la Chatterjee, Calcutta: Visva-Bharati, 1968.

The Golden Boat, Trans. Bhabani Bhattacharya, Bombay: Jaico Publishing House, 1956.

Wings of Death. Trans. Aurobindo Bose. London: John Murry, 1960.

II. Other Writings of Rabindranath Tagore

A Tagore Reader, Ed. Amiya Chakravarty, New York: Macmillan, 1961.

Angel of *Surplus*. Ed. Sisirkumar Ghose. Calcutta: Visva-Bharati, 1978.

Bharati, Nos. 1287, 1288, 1289 and 1789.

Creative Unity, London: Macmillan and Co., Limited, 1925.

Glimpses of Bengal, Madras: macmillan Pocket Tagore Edition, 1985.

Lectures and Addresses by Rabindranath Tagore, London: Macmillan, 1985.

Letters from Russia, Calcutta: Visva-Bharati, 1960.

My Boyhood Days, Trans. Marjorie Sykes. Calcutta: Visa-Bharati, 1986.

Nationalism, Madras: Macmillan, 1985.

On the Edges of Time. Calcutta: Orient Longmens, 1958.

One Hundred Poems of Kabir, (Trans.), Madras: Macmillan Pocket Tagore edition, 1988.

Personality, Madras: Macmillan Pocket Tagore Edition, 1985.

Rabindra Rachanavali, Vols. I (a), II, III and XI.

Reminiscences. Delhi: Macmillan, 1983.

Sadhana. Calcutta: Macmillan and Co. Limited, 1946.

The Diary of a Wesward Voyage. Calcutta: Asia Publishing House, 1962.

The Religion of an Artist. Calcutta: Visva-Bharati, 1963.

The Religion of Man. London: George Allen a Unwin Limited, 1958.

Towards Universal Man. Bombay: Asia Publishing House, 1967.

III. Biographical and Critical Studies on Rabindranath Tagore

Anand, Mulk Raj. *The Volcano: Some Comments on the Development of Rabindranath Tagore's Aesthetic Theories and Art Practice*. Baroda: Maharaja Sayaji Rao University, 1967.

Aronson, A. *Rabindranath Through Western Eyes*, Allahabad: Indian Press, 1934.

Bhattacharya, S. *Tagore and the World*. Calcutta: Das Gupta & Co., 1961.

Bhattacharje, M.M. *Rabindranath Tagore: Poet and Thinker*, Delhi: Kitaba Mahal, 1961.

Banerjee, *Hiranmy How Thou Singest My Master*: Calcutta: Orient Longmans, 1961.

Banerjee, *The Humanism of Tagore*, Prasaranga: University of Mysore, 1968.

Banerji, Dr. Srikumar, *Phases of Tagore's Poetry*. Prasaranga: University of Mysore, 1973.

Bose, Buddhdeva, *Tagore: Portrait of a Poet*. University of Bombay, 1962.

------, *An Acre of Green Grass*. Calcutta: Orient Longmans, 1948.

Chakravarty, B.C. *Rabindranath Tagore: His Mind and Art*. New Delhi: Young India Publications, 1971.

Chandra Sekharan, K. *Tagore and Master Spirit*, Masulipatnam: Trieni Press, 1961.

Chattarji, Suniti Kumar, *Lectures on Rabindranath Tagore*, Aurangabad: Marathwada University, 1965.

Chaudhary, Prabas Jiban, *Tagore on Literature and Aesthetics*, Calcutta: Rabindra Bharati, 1965.

Cuthbertson, Carol. *Tagore an Artist*. Calcutta: Visva-Bharati, 1968.

Das, Prafulla Chandra, *Tagore: The Poet of Light*. Cuttack, 1962.

Devi, Maitraye, *Tagore by Fire Side*, Calcutta; Rupa & Co., 1961.

Ghose, Sisirkumar. *Later Poems of Tagore*. Bombay: Asia Publishing House, 1961.

-------, "Angel of Surplus – A Note on Tagorean Aesthetics," *Critical Essays on Indian Writing in English*, Eds. M.K. Naik, S.K. Desai & G.S. Amur, Madras: The Macmillan Co. of India Ltd., 1977.

Gupta, Rameshwar. *The Essential Tagore*, Rajasthan: Banasthali, 1961.

Introduction to Tagore (Ed.), Calcutta: Visva-Bharati, 1983.

Kantak, V.Y. "Tagore's Views on Poetry and Art", *The Banasthali Patrika*, No. 13 (July, 1969), pp. 1-17.

Khanolkar, G.D. *The Lute and the Plough: A Life of Rabindranath Tagore*. Trans. Thomas Gay. Bombay: The Book Centre Private Ltd., 1963.

Kriplani, Krishna, *Tagore: A Life*, New Delhi: Malancha, 1961.

Mukherji, S.B. *The Poety of Tagore*, New Delhi: Vikas Publishing House, 1977.

Mukherji, Dhurjati Prasad, *Tagore – A Study*, Calcutta: Manisha, 1972.

Mukherji, Prabhat Kumar, *Life of Tagore*, Trans. Sisirkumar Ghose. New Delhi: Indian Book Co., 1975.

Muley, D.S *Rabindranath Tagore's Poetry*. Jabalpur: Universal Book Depot, 1964.

Narvane, V.S. *An Introduction to Rabindranath Tagore*, Madras: Macmillan, 1977.

Radhakrishnan, S. *The Philosophy of Rabindranath Tagore*, Baroda: Good Companions, 1958.

Ray, Benoy Gopal, *The Philosophy of Rabindranath Tagore*, Bombay: Hind Kitabs, 1949.

Rhys, Ernest, *Rabindranath Tagore*. London: Macmillan, 1963.

Sen Gupta, S.C. *Rabindranath Tagore: Homagc from Visva-Bharati, Santiniketan: Visva-Bharati*, 1962.

------, *Some Aspects of the Poetry of Tagore*, Prasaranga: University of Mysore, 1970.

------, *The Great Sentinel*, Calcutta, 1948.

Sharma, K.K. (Ed.), *Indo-English Literature*, Ghaziabad: Vimal Prakashan, 1977.

-------, *Rabindranath Tagore's Aesthetics*, New Delh: Abhinav Publications, 1988.

Sharma, T.R. (Ed.), *Essays on Rabindranath Tagore*, Ghaziabad: Vimal Prakashan, 1987.

------,*Perspectives on Rabindranath Tagore*, Ghaziabad: Vimal Prakashan, 1986.

Singh, Baldev, *Tagore and the Romantic Ideology*, Calcutta: Orient Longomans, 1963.

Singh, Ajai, *Rabindranath Tagore: His Imagery and Ideas*, Ghaziabad: Vimal Prakashan, 1984.

Sastri, K.S.R. *Sri Rabindranath Tagore*, Madras, 1916.

Sykes, Marjorie, *Rabindranath Tagore*, Calcutta, 1943.

Thompson, Edward J. *Rabindranath Tagore: His Life and Work*. Calcutta:Y.M.C.A. Publishing House, 1961.

------,*Rabindranath Tagore: Poet and Dramatist*. London: Oxford University Press, 1948.

IV. Others Works Consulted

Abrams, M.H. *The Mirror and the Lamp: Romantic Theory and the Critical Tradition*, New York: Oxford University Press Paperback, 1976.

Alex, Preminger, *Encyclopaedia of Poetry and Poetics*, Princeton University Press, 1965.

Aristotle, *Aristotle's Theory of Poetry and Fine Art*, Trans. S.H. Butcher, Ludhiana: Kalyani Publishers, 1974.

Bicknell, Herman, Hafiz of Shiraz: A Selection from His Poem. Tehran: *Imperial Organization for Social Services*, 1976.

Bhagavad Gita, The. Trans, Juan Mascaro. Penguin Books, 1974.

Boulton, Marjorie, *The Anatomy of Poetry*. Ludhiana: Kalyani, Publishers, 1979.

Bowra, C.M. *Inspiration and Poetry*. London: Macmillan End Co., 1955.

------*The Romantic Imagination*. London: Oxford University Press, 1964.

Brown, Brain, *The Wisdom of Hindus*. Delhi: Heritage Publishers, 1973.

Briggs, Harold E. *The Complete Poetry and Selected Prose of John Keats*. The Modern Library, 1951.

Carritt, E.F. *The Theory of Beauty*. London: Methuen & Co., 1914.

Caudwell Christopher. *Illusion and reality*. London: Lawrence & Wshart, 1950.

Croce, Benedetto, Aesthetic. New Delhi: Rupa & Co., 1962.

Dwivedi, Acharya Hazari Prasad, *Kabir*. Delhi: Rajkamal Prakashan, 1971.

Fromm, Erich. *The Art of Loving*. London: Unwin Books, 1975.

Frye, Northrop, *Anatomy of Criticism*, Princeton University Press, 1957.

Gitagovinda of Jayadeva: *Love Song of the Dark Lord*, Ed. and Trans. Barbara Stoler Miller, Delhi: Motilal Banarsidass, 1984.

Gokak, V.K. An Integral View of Poetry, New Delhi: Abhinav Publications, 1975.

Hutchinson, Thomas (Ed.). *The Poetical Works of William Wordsworth.* London: Oxford University Press, 1946.

---(Ed.) *The Complete Poetrical Works of Percy Bysshe Shelley,* London: Oxford University Press, 1956.

Iyengar, K.R.S. *Indian Writing in English,* Bombay: Asia Publishing House, 1962.

Kreiger, Murray. *The New Apologists for Poetry.* University of Minnesota Press, 1956.

Mammat, Kavyaprakash. Trans. Ganga Nath Jha, Allahabad, 1926.

Morgan, Douglas N. Love, Plato, *The Bible and Freud.* Bombay: Jaico Publishing House, 1966.

Naik, M.K., Desai, S.K. & Amur, G.S. (Eds.) *Critical Essays on Indian Writing in English.* Madras: The Macmillan Co. of India Ltd., 1977.

Naik, M.K. (Ed.), *Perspectives on Indian Poetry in English,* New Delhi: Abhinav Publications, 1984.

----- (Ed.), *Aspects of Indian Writing in English.* Madras: Macmillan, 1979.

----, *A History of Indian English Literature,* Delhi: Sahitya Akademy, 1982.

Narasimhaiah, C.D. (Ed.), *Indian Literature of the Past Fifty Years* (1917-1967), Prasaranga: University of Mysore, 1970.

---(Ed.), *Literary Criticism: European and Indian Traditions,* University of Mysore,1968.

Nehru, Jawahar Lal. *The Discovery of India,* Calcutta: The Signet Press, 1946.

Pandey, Kanti Chandra, *Comparative Aesthetics* (Vols. I & II), Banaras: Chowkhamba Sanskrit Series, 1956.

Reynolds, Myra, *The Treatment of Nature in English Poetry*, Chicago, 1896.

Shirazi, Syed Abul Kasim, Injuyi (Ed.), *Diwan-i-Khwajeh Hafiz Shirazi*, Tehran: Sazman-i-intesharat-i-Javidan, Solar, 1363.

Shukla, Acharya Ram Chandra, *History of Hindi Literature*, Kashi: Nagri Pracharni Sabha, 1962.

Tagore, Maharshi Devendranath, *The Autobiography*, Trans, Satyendranath Tagore and Indira Devi, London: Mcmillan and Co. Limited, 1961.

Trilling, Lionel, The Liberal Imagination, New York, 1955.

Upanishads, The Liberal Imagination, New York, 1955.

Upanishads, The Trans. Juan Mascaro, Penguin Books, 1974.

Wellek, R. and Warren, Austin, *Theory of Literature*, Penguin Books, 1963.

Index

T

U

V

W

***